# The Mount Sinai Text

## (The Ten Commandments)

OSCAR C. JOHNSON PHD

ISBN: 978-1-965951-00-2 (sc)
ISBN: 978-1-965951-01-9 (ebk)

Seraphim Global Media LLC
155 Willowbrook Blvd Ste 110
Wayne, NJ 07470
848 800 6538
info@seraphimgml.com

# Contents

# PREFACE

I am saddened. I am saddened because the majority of Americans fail to acknowledge the commandments that God has given us. The sad thing is that ignorance of these commandments can have a significant impact on one's salvation. This ignorance or frank defiance of the commandments by most every encounter I experience has brought me to tears on multiple occasions.

Preachers are teaching that belief in Jesus and accepting Him as one's personal savior is all that is needed for salvation. Yes, the Lord grants us salvation by His grace, through faith, but what preachers are not teaching is that one can lose their salvation.

> [17]Thus also faith by itself, if it does not have works, is dead.
>
> [18]But someone will say, "You have faith, and I have works." Show me your faith without [a] your works, and I will show you my faith by [b]my works.
>
> [19]You believe that there is one God. You do well. Even the demons believe—and tremble!
>
> [20]But do you want to know, O foolish man, that faith without works is [c] dead?
>
> [21]Was not Abraham our father justified by works when he offered Isaac his son on the altar?
>
> [22]Do you see that faith was working together with his works, and by works faith was made [d] perfect?

[23]And the Scripture was fulfilled which says,

"Abraham believed God, and it was [e] accounted to him for righteousness." And he was called the friend of God.

[24]You see then that a man is justified by works, and not by faith only. (James 2:17-24 NKJV)

Many denominations, Christian and Non-Christian, quote the Apostle James contradicting the words of the Apostle Paul. The emphasis on works is so prevalent that many people believe that they can only be saved by "good works". Where works are essential for the maintenance of one's salvation, it is not the criteria that determines one's salvation.

The verse that many Pastors and Priest quote to convince their parishioners the importance of works is,

[20]But do you want to know, O foolish man, that faith without works is [c] dead? (James 2:20 NKJV)

This appears straightforward, without works, faith is dead. However, evaluating the full context of the Apostle James message shows us two verses later that Verse 20 is taken out of correct context.

[22]Do you see that faith was working together with his works, and by works faith was made [d] perfect? (James 2:22 NKJV)

As one can see, faith precedes works. The Apostle Paul is unambiguous about the relationship between faith and works.

[8]For by grace you have been saved through faith, and that not of yourselves; *it is* the gift of God,

[9]not of works, lest anyone should boast. (Ephesians 2:8-9 NKJV)

**²⁸For we maintain that a person is justified by faith apart from the works of the law. (Romans 3:28 NIV)**

Therefore, there is no contradiction between the Apostle James and the Apostle Paul. The Apostle James is telling the Twelve Tribes that works are important for the maintenance of our salvation after our transformation into justification, that is, salvation.

Obedience is a major theme throughout Scripture. The Apostle John tells us that "we know that we have come to know Him" (1 John 2:3 NIV). John is not saying our salvation is conditional on obedience but obedience is evidence of our salvation. This evidence is manifested in the way one lives one's life. If they know God, their lives change. They live by the commandments of the Lord.

This is the problem for our society today. Many people who profess to be Christian can't explain what is involved in the life choice they are professing. Most believe that they only need a belief in Jesus and that He died for our sins as the only requirement for salvation. This same group also have no idea that being obedient to the commandments of God are part of the requirements also.

Unfortunately, still is the group of people that say that they believe in God and only need to be a good person to get to heaven. This group clearly does not understand the concept of attaining salvation or the gospel of Jesus. Without this understanding, an understanding of the significance of the 10 Commandments is also absent.

The Barna Group (a private, non-partisan for-profit research group in Ventura, California who conduct and analyze primary research to understand cultural trends related to values, beliefs, attitudes and behaviors), found that 88% of all American households contain a Bible. The average is 4.7 copies per household. Even with the abundance of Bibles in homes, there is little understanding of what it reveals. It appears that rather than trying to understand the Word of God, people have Bibles, for show. Unsurprisingly, this would explain the lack of knowledge of the commandments of God.

A USA Today poll says the majority of Americans don't believe that the 10 Commandments are not incapable of change. In this same poll, 60% of Americans could not name 5 of the 10 Commandments. (Grossman, 2007) In fact, only 14% can name all 10 Commandments. Yet 78 % favor public display of the Commandments. Additionally, 56% of the survey respondents proclaimed to being "pro-Bible" meaning they think it is the actual or inspired of God with no errors. You would think that this much belief in the Bible would inspire more study of its contents.

A study conducted by the Deseret News of Salt Lake City, Utah, between 2011 and 2013 revealed that the 19% of American adults believe the Bible is "just another book of teachings written by men that contains stories and advice". The same study revealed greater than 90% of Americans believed some commandments were relevant to modern society while others were not applicable. The ones that still were morally important included the commandments regarding murder, stealing, and lying and of these 60% believed there is flexibility in lying. To exaggerate was nominally accepted when considered a "white lie". However, the more religious a person was, the less they would accept any lie. This trend is increasingly evident in Millennials, who have a tendency to identify with the groups called "nones". These are people who follow no religion at all.

Professor Mark Chaves, department of Sociology, Religious Studies and Divinity at Duke University, believes that Millennials are not necessarily comfortable with topics such as murder or stealing, they are just more uncomfortable with topics on religion. He states, "I think with their response they are saying, 'I'm not a religious person, so the Ten Commandments aren't for me at all.'"

British Christians feel the first four commandments are not relevant in today's world. These are the commandments regarding our relationship with God. A YouGov survey revealed:

- 44% believe the 2nd Commandment, idol worship, is not an important commandment, with only 31% saying that people should not worship idols. 20% say it is still an important commandment

- Only 20% of Britons believe in the Christian God monopoly being relevant. "I am the Lord thy God", the 1st Commandment, is one of the least important commandments.

- 23% believe that the 3rd Commandment is relevant as the majority of the population have a disregard for the used of the word "God". Using the Lord's name in vain is a norm in casual conversation.

- Britons believe the 4th Commandment, keeping the Sabbath Day holy is the least of all the commandments. Only 19% believe that keeping Sunday holy is an important principle to live by. Of the 19%, 31% were Christian.

(Smith, 2017)

Modern society views the 10 Commandments as a set of antiquated rules that pertained to the Jewish people of the Old Testament. Many believe that these were replaced by new commandments by Jesus Christ. This is incorrect.

This book is for those who have ever wondered about the 10 Commandments. It is my attempt to perform an immersed critique into the deeper meanings of the commandments of God. I hope to reveal the importance of the commandments.

- For Christians and non-Christians alike
- How relevant are they to modern life
- Who do they pertain to
- Why we must follow them

- What Jesus said
- When they were conceived
- Who is the Author
- Regarding our salvation

I am a Christian who contemplates the Word of God every day. I think about things that could bring someone closer to God and Jesus. For the most part, the things I write about are from my mind. For the most part it is written in prose so that anyone can understand. They are my opinions and may not represent the views of others. However, I do read many other authors and cite them for the use of their intellect. In no way do I want to mislead anyone into thinking that I am a pastor, apostle, minister or priest. Nor am I a theologian. However, I do have a passion for God, Jesus and the written Word. I write to share my thoughts with fellow Christians who sincerely believe the 10 Commandments to be the apogee of divine guidance and maybe, just maybe, attract the attention of a non-Christian who may have questions regarding the Word of God.

**¹⁷Ye shall diligently keep the commandments of the LORD your God, and his testimonies, and his statutes, which he hath commanded thee. (Deuteronomy 6:17 KJV)**

# INTRODUCTION

According to Jewish tradition, there are 613 laws which are the whole body of the Mosaic legislation that they are to follow. These are the Laws of Moses. The laws were given to the people of Israel by God using Moses as His mediator. This body of laws contained all the ceremonies, rituals and obligations regarding their relationship with God. The laws were also referred to as the Mosaic Covenant. The Pharisees (religious leaders) were experts of the Laws of Moses and advocated strict observance and practice of these laws to attain salvation. The Mosaic Laws are a summation of the divine laws of the 10 Commandments.

To summarize the Laws of Moses,

I.  Laws of worship
    A)  Idolatry & paganism
        a)  No idols
        b)  No sacrificing to other gods
        c)  No consorting with other peoples
        d)  No sorcery or augury
        e)  No human sacrifices
        f)  No pagan superstitions
        g)  No cult prostitution

    B)  Sacrifices, offerings, tithes, and vows
        a)  Sacrifices
        b)  Burnt offerings
        c)  Grain offerings
        d)  Fellowship offerings
        e)  Sin offerings
        f)  Guilt offerings

g) Acceptable & unacceptable offerings
h) Giving of produce
i) Giving of firstborn
j) Tithes
k) Vows
l) Nazirite vow

C) Priestly duties & privileges
   a) Consecration of priesthood
   b) Purity of priesthood
   c) Priest's duties in sacrificing
   d) Rules for killing sacrifices
   e) The eating of holy things by priests
   f) Duties of Levites
   g) Levitical cities

D) Special religious occasions
   a) Jubilee year
   b) Sabbath year
   c) Feast days
   d) Day of Atonement
   e) Sabbath day

E) Special, religious articles
   a) Tabernacle and furnishings
   b) Revering the sanctuary
   c) Place for the altar
   d) Kind of altar
   e) Altar on Mt. Ebal
   f) Tassels of remembrance

F) Other religious duties
   a) Consecration of the people
   b) Loving God and teaching Him to children
   c) True and false prophets
   d) Putting God to the test

e) Reviling God
f) Punishment for blasphemy
g) No mixing of breeds, grain, cloth
h) Those excluded from the LORD's assembly
i) Acceptance of Egyptians and Edomites
j) Confirm the Law by doing it
k) Blessings of obedience
l) Curses of disobedience
m) Keeping the covenant
n) Promise of restoration
o) Choice: life or death

II. Laws of physical purity

A) Foods
a) Clean and unclean animals
b) No eating of blood
c) Eating sacrifices on the same day
d) No eating of meat torn by beasts

B) Diseases
a) Leprosy
b) Isolation of unclean
c) Camp sanitation

C) Normal human processes
a) Secretions of man
b) Secretions of woman
c) No sexual relations during menstrual period
d) Purification of woman after childbirth

III. Laws concerning business dealings & politics

D) Land ownership
a) Division of the land
b) No removing of landmarks

c) Safety requirement for buildings
d) Inheritance rights
e) Levirate marriage
f) Redemption of property

E) Slaves & hired servants
   a) Concerning slaves
   b) Redemption of slaves
   c) Oppressing a hired servant

F) Ecology
   a) Preserving the fruit trees
   b) Preserving the wildlife
   c) Preserving the domesticated animals

G) Lending laws
   a) Things taken in pledge
   b) No charging of interest

H) Business practices
   a) Using just weights & measures
   b) Restitution

I) Civil justice
   a) No perverting of justice
   b) Oppressing the widow, orphan, or poor
   c) Oppressing the stranger
   d) Oppressing one's neighbor
   e) Oppressing the physically disabled
   f) Judicial system

J) Laws protecting the poor
   a) Oppressing the widow, orphan, or poor
   b) Gleanings for the poor
   c) Rights to eat of anyone's crops

K) Cruelty

L) Military laws
    a) Choosing a king
    b) Military service
    c) Besieging hostile cities
    d) Command to exterminate Amalek

M) Liability for accidents

IV. Laws of morality

N) Sex crimes
    a) Incest
    b) Adultery
    c) Homosexual practice
    d) Cross-dressing
    e) Fornication with a slave
    f) Bestiality
    g) Seduction of a virgin
    h) Rape laws
    i) Making one's daughter into a prostitute
    j) Seizing a man's sex organs to prevent a beating

O) Marriage, divorce, & remarriage
    a) Marriage of free to slave
    b) Marriage of free to captive
    c) No remarrying of original spouse after intervening marriage
    d) Trial of the suspected adulteress
    e) Trial of the bride suspected of pre-marital promiscuity

P) Violent crimes & their punishments
    a) Murder & other violent acts
    b) Atoning for the unknown murderer's guilt
    c) Cities of refuge

d)	Kidnapping a man to enslave him
e)	Punishment of forty stripes
f)	Burial of an executed criminal
g)	No hatred for one's brother
h)	No personal vengeance

Q)	Other offenses
a)	Testimony in trials
b)	Reviling a ruler
c)	Stoning of a rebellious son
d)	Treatment of enemies

R)	Crimes that carried the death penalty
a)	Striking or reviling a parent
b)	Blasphemy
c)	Sabbath breaking
d)	Witchcraft
e)	Adultery
f)	Rape
g)	Incestuous & homosexual relations
h)	Kidnapping
i)	Idolatry
j)	Touching Mount Sinai
k)	Murder

Steve Singleton: Multi-Index to the Law of Moses.
E-book (2007-005)

In actuality, there are only 603 Laws of Moses. The first 10 are excluded because they were given to the people of Israel directly from God.

**[18]When the LORD finished speaking to Moses on Mount Sinai, he gave him the two tablets of the covenant law, the tablets of stone inscribed by the finger of God. (Exodus 31:18 NIV)**

The 10 Commandments are the moral laws of God. These laws existed from the beginning of creation. They were given to explain our relationship to God, our relationship to our elder family members and our relationship to our community and the world at large.

Jesus tells us that He did not come to abolish the moral Laws of God, but to affirm them. He also explained the futility of relying on the Laws of Moses for salvation. This was also a major part of the Apostle Paul's ministry. He educated Jews and Gentiles regarding sin and the law.

**[19]Now we know that whatever the law says, it says to those who are under the law, so that every mouth may be silenced and the whole world held accountable to God.**

**[20]Therefore no one will be declared righteous in God's sight by the works of the law; rather, through the law we become conscious of our sin. (Romans 3:19-20 NIV)**

The Apostle Paul taught that God gave Man Mosaic Law to identify sin. This didn't mean that the laws were bad, only that they required strict adherence. Even if one could live by the Mosaic Laws, they would still not attain salvation by works alone. Paul explains in his letter to his protege´ Timothy the purpose of the law.

**[8]We know that the law is good if one uses it properly.**

**[9]We also know that the law is made not for the righteous but for lawbreakers and rebels, the ungodly and sinful, the unholy and irreligious, for those who kill their fathers or mothers, for murderers,**

**[10]for the sexually immoral, for those practicing homosexuality, for slave traders and liars and**

**perjurers—and for whatever else is contrary to the sound doctrine (1 Timothy 1:8-10 NIV)**

"We Are Not Sinners Because We Sin, We Sin Because We are Sinners". (Sproul, 2016) The Laws of God, the 10 Commandments, are our roadmap for moral and ethical living. This is echoed in the New Testament by the Apostle Paul in all 15 of his letters.

Henceforth, we have God's moral laws. If we follow them, we don't need the Laws of Moses or need to be concerned about them. Accepting Jesus changes our hearts and make it very easy to live by the Lord's moral laws. When He died on the cross, He not only died for our sins but also took our sinful nature away.

Jesus said:

**[21]Whoever has my commands and keeps them is the one who loves me. The one who loves me will be loved by my Father, and I too will love them and show myself to them." (John 14:21 NKJV)**

# HISTORY

Most Biblical scholars believe the 10 Commandments were written between 1600 B.C.E. and 1300 B.C.E with 1430 B.C.E. to 1450 B.C.E. being favored. However, there are scholars that dispute not only when they were written, but also by whom. There are many modern scholars who suggest that the commandments presented by Moses were influenced by the "best ideas" of various sources from the cultures of the area and included God inspired and pagan ideas.

Biblically and historically, it is accepted that Moses presented the 10 Commandments to the people of Israel. This occurred around 1448 B.C.E. God had delivered the Jewish people from slavery in Egypt to be solely devoted to Him. It was through obedience to God's laws that the people of Israel could complete its role as a holy people and nation.

The academic controversy stems from questions about who actually created the commandments. The Bible tells us that God wrote the original 10 Commandment Himself. Modern religious scholars question this biblical authorship.

Since Moses was raised and educated in Egypt by the educators of the Pharaoh, he was familiar with the ancient laws of the Hittites and Egyptians. Both of these sources were of pagan origin and were part of Moses spiritual education in the Kemetic Spirituality tradition. It is this education combined with the Hebrew Bible that may have inspired Moses while constructing the commandments.

Hittites

Hittite documents discovered from the 14th Century B.C.E. and 13th Century B.C.E. present sections of clay tablets discussing rulership, benefits to the people and description of obligations. Some of these laws are said to be incorporated into the construction of the 10 Commandments. These laws may have been much older as archaeological findings have been found of the Hittites from 2000 B.C.E. The Hittites were pagans and polytheistic worshiping multiple animal gods. It was possible that they worshiped thousands of gods. Their gods were also imperfect. They required food and companionship. They lacked omniscience, omnipotence and omnipresence. Even with their faults, they were superior to humans. Throughout Old Testament Jewish history and text, Hittites were integrated into the Jewish and Egyptian society. They shared their religious beliefs with Egyptians and Jews.

Egyptians

Moses was extremely versed in the laws and religion of the Egyptian people. The Egyptian Book of the Dead, the template of laws established mentions the same rules as the 10 Commandments. Originating from concepts depicted in tomb paintings, the Book of the Dead dates back to the Third Dynasty of Egypt (2670 B.C.E. - 2613 B.C.E). By the 12th Dynasty (1991 B.C.E. - 1802 B.C.E.) the writings and illustrations were written on papyrus.

Many modern scholars contend that the Book of the Dead was most influential regarding the content of the commandments. In this text are the '42 Negative Confessions' found in the Papyrus of ANI and the Papyrus of NU. 8 out of 10 commandments can be found in the confessions. 'The 42 Confessions' are considered the Whole Law or the Law of Ma'at.

1.  Hail, Usekh-nemmt, who comest forth from Anu, I have not committed sin.

2.  Hail, Hept-khet, who comest forth from Kher-aha, I have not committed robbery with violence.

3.  Hail, Fenti, who comest forth from Khemenu, I have not stolen.

4.  Hail, Am-khaibit, who comest forth from Qernet, I have not slain men and women.

5. Hail, Neha-her, who comest forth from Rasta, I have not stolen grain.

6. Hail, Ruruti, who comest forth from Heaven, I have not purloined offerings.

7. Hail, Arfi-em-khet, who comest forth from Suat, I have not stolen the property of God.

8. Hail, Neba, who comest and goest, I have not uttered lies.

9. Hail, Set-qesu, who comest forth from Hensu, I have not carried away food.

10. Hail, Utu-nesert, who comest forth from Het-ka-Ptah, I have not uttered curses.

11. Hail, Qerrti, who comest forth from Amentet, I have not committed adultery.

12. Hail, Hraf-haf, who comest forth from thy cavern, I have made none to weep.

13. Hail, Basti, who comest forth from Bast, I have not eaten the heart.

14. Hail, Ta-retiu, who comest forth from the night, I have not attacked any man.

15. Hail, Unem-snef, who comest forth from the execution chamber, I am not a man of deceit.

16. Hail, Unem-besek, who comest forth from Mabit, I have not stolen cultivated land.

17. Hail, Neb-Maat, who comest forth from Maati, I have not been an eavesdropper.

18. Hail, Tenemiu, who comest forth from Bast, I have not slandered anyone.

19. Hail, Sertiu, who comest forth from Anu, I have not been angry without just cause.

20. Hail, Tutu, who comest forth from Ati, I have not debauched the wife of any man.

21. Hail, Uamenti, who comest forth from the Khebt chamber, I have not debauched the wives of other men.

22. Hail, Maa-antuf, who comest forth from Per-Menu, I have not polluted myself.

23. Hail, Her-uru, who comest forth from Nehatu, I have terrorized none.

24. Hail, Khemiu, who comest forth from Kaui, I have not transgressed the law.

25. Hail, Shet-kheru, who comest forth from Urit, I have not been angry.

26. Hail, Nekhenu, who comest forth from Heqat, I have not shut my ears to the words of truth.

27. Hail, Kenemti, who comest forth from Kenmet, I have not blasphemed.

28. Hail, An-hetep-f, who comest forth from Sau, I am not a man of violence.

29. Hail, Sera-kheru, who comest forth from Unaset, I have not been a stirrer up of strife.

30. Hail, Neb-heru, who comest forth from Netchfet, I have not acted with undue haste.

31. Hail, Sekhriu, who comest forth from Uten, I have not pried into other's matters.

32. Hail, Neb-abui, who comest forth from Sauti, I have not multiplied my words in speaking.

33. Hail, Nefer-Tem, who comest forth from Het-ka-Ptah, I have wronged none, I have done no evil.

34. Hail, Tem-Sepu, who comest forth from Tetu, I have not worked witchcraft against the king.

35. Hail, Ari-em-ab-f, who comest forth from Tebu, I have never stopped the flow of water of a neighbor.

36. Hail, Ahi, who comest forth from Nu, I have never raised my voice.

37. Hail, Uatch-rekhit, who comest forth from Sau, I have not cursed God.

38. Hail, Neheb-ka, who comest forth from thy cavern, I have not acted with arrogance.

39. Hail, Neheb-nefert, who comest forth from thy cavern, I have not stolen the bread of the gods.

40. Hail, Tcheser-tep, who comest forth from the shrine, I have not carried away the khenfu cakes from the spirits of the dead.

41. Hail, An-af, who comest forth from Maati, I have not snatched away the bread of the child, nor treated with contempt the god of my city.

42. Hail, Hetch-abhu, who comest forth from Ta-she, I have not slain the cattle belonging to the god.

> Papyrus of Ani, The Egyptian Book of the Dead 1240 BCE. Translated by E.A. Wallis Budge.

In a more palatable format,

1. I have not committed sin.

2. I have not committed robbery with violence.

3. I have not stolen.

4. I have not slain men and women.

5. I have not stolen grain.

6. I have not purloined offerings.

7. I have not stolen the property of God.

8. I have not uttered lies.

9. I have not carried away food.

10. I have not uttered curses.

11. I have not committed adultery, I have not lain with men.

12. I have made none to weep.

13. I have not eaten the heart.

14. I have not attacked any man.

15. I am not a man of deceit.

16. I have not stolen cultivated land.

17. I have not been an eavesdropper.

18. I have not slandered.

19. I have not been angry without just cause.

20. I have not debauched the wife of any man.

21. I have not debauched the wife of any man.

22. I have not polluted myself.

23. I have terrorized none.

24. I have not transgressed the law.

25. I have not been wroth.

26. I have not shut my ears to the words of truth.

27. I have not blasphemed.

28. I am not a man of violence.

29. I have not been a stirrer up of strife.

30. I have not acted with undue haste.

31. I have not pried into matters.

32. I have not multiplied my words in speaking.

33. I have wronged none, I have done no evil.

34. I have not worked witchcraft against the king.

35. I have never stopped the flow of water.

36. I have never raised my voice.

37. I have not cursed God.

38. I have not acted with arrogance.

39. I have not stolen the bread of the gods.

40. I have not carried away the khenfu cakes from the Spirits of the dead.

41. I have not snatched away the bread of the child, nor treated with contempt the god of my city.

42. I have not slain the cattle belonging to the god.

The '42 Confessions' are also known as the Laws of Ma'at. Ma'at is the Egyptian goddess of Truth, Justice and Order. Ma'at is the daughter of Ra, the sun god and Torath, the god of writing. The ancient Egyptians worshiped her by living according to the values of justice, order and harmony. She is depicted with an ostrich feather on her head. This feather was important in the determination of one's fate after death.

When a person died, their soul is immediately transported to the underworld, a place called Du'at. It is there that their soul would enter the Hall of Two Truths where they go through a process called the Judgment of Osiris. In this process, their heart is weighed on a golden scale against Ma'at's Feather of Truth. This is done in front of a panel of 42 judges led by Osiris, the god of the dead. This panel would determine the worthiness of the soul. If the heart is heavier than the feather, the person is confined to Du'at for all eternity. If the heart is lighter than or equal to the feather, the person is welcomed into the afterlife, the Field of Reeds. People strived to live according to Ma'at for a chance to enter the afterlife.

The Book of the Dead has been considered the predecessor of the Bible with the '42 Confessions' being the forefather of the Law of Moses, ergo, the 10 Commandments. The allegation is that the ancient Hebrew writers plagiarized pagan documents written by Hittites or Egyptians to create the Law of Moses and the 10 Commandments. These theories regarding the 10 Commandments are rejected by religious conservatives who believe that God spoke the 10 Commandments to Moses who recorded them as part of the Pentateuch, the first 5 books of the Bible.

# THE VIEW OF
# THE BELIEVER

The 10 Commandments (the Decalogue) are ten laws given to Moses by God to present to the people of Israel 133 days after their exodus from Egypt. Of the 316 Laws of Moses, these 10 are set apart and special. The 10 Commandments are considered to be apodictic laws, laws that are absolute. Of the 613 laws found in the Torah (the Hebrew Bible) these are the most important of the laws.

The people of Israel had been in the Desert of Sin for 3 months after their exodus when God told them to gather at the base of the mountain Sinai and prepare themselves. He gave them 3 days to prepare. God appeared in a cloud with lighting and thunder. This scared the people who then implored Moses to speak to them for God because they feared that if God spoke to them directly, they would die. God revealed his covenant to the people through Moses and then called Moses to join him on the mountain. 40 days later Moses returned with the commandments. It was during the period of the 1st Passover after Egypt.

The 10 Commandments are a summary of the 613 commandments of Jewish tradition that were Old Testament law found in the Torah. (Drazi, 2009) The Torah is the law of God as revealed to Moses and recorded in the first five books of the Hebrew scriptures (the Pentateuch). These laws are referred to as the "Law of Moses" and are believed to be penned by him as inspired by God. The purpose was to guide the people of Israel into a life of practical holiness. The Ten Commandments offer basic rules of behavior for spiritual and moral living. For 400 years the people of Israel had no law other than that of the Pharaoh of Egypt. For 400 years the people of Israel lived as slaves, restricted in the worship of their God.

In the Bible, the original and most accepted version of the 10 Commandments is presented in the Exodus 20:1-17.

[1]And God spake all these words, saying,

[2]I am the LORD thy God, which have brought thee out of the land of Egypt, out of the house of bondage.

[3]Thou shalt have no other gods before me.

[4]Thou shalt not make unto thee any graven image, or any likeness of any thing that is in heaven above, or that is in the earth beneath, or that is in the water under the earth.

[5]Thou shalt not bow down thyself to them, nor serve them: for I the LORD thy God am a jealous God, visiting the iniquity of the fathers upon the children unto the third and fourth generation of them that hate me;

[6]And shewing mercy unto thousands of them that love me, and keep my commandments.

[7]Thou shalt not take the name of the LORD thy God in vain; for the LORD will not hold him guiltless that taketh his name in vain.

[8]Remember the sabbath day, to keep it holy.

[9]Six days shalt thou labour, and do all thy work:

[10]But the seventh day is the sabbath of the LORD thy God: in it thou shalt not do any work, thou, nor thy son, nor thy daughter, thy manservant, nor thy maidservant, nor thy cattle, nor thy stranger that is within thy gates:

[11]For in six days the LORD made heaven and earth, the sea, and all that in them is, and rested the seventh day: wherefore the LORD blessed the sabbath day, and hallowed it.

**[12]Honour thy father and thy mother: that thy days may be long upon the land which the LORD thy God giveth thee.**

**[13]Thou shalt not kill.**

**[14]Thou shalt not commit adultery.**

**[15]Thou shalt not steal.**

**[16]Thou shalt not bear false witness against thy neighbour.**

**[17]Thou shalt not covet thy neighbour's house, thou shalt not covet thy neighbour's wife, nor his manservant, nor his maidservant, nor his ox, nor his ass, nor any thing that is thy neighbour's. (Exodus 20:1-17 KJV)**

Forty years later, five weeks prior to his death, Moses assembled the people of Israel to give them a final parting speech. The 5th and 6th Books of Deuteronomy contain his restatement of commandments from God and the tenets of Judaism, beginning with the reiteration of the 10 Commandments. This version of the commandments is presented in Deuteronomy 5:6-21.

**[6]I am the LORD thy God, which brought thee out of the land of Egypt, from the house of bondage.**

**[7]Thou shalt have none other gods before me.**

**[8]Thou shalt not make thee any graven image, or any likeness of any thing that is in heaven above, or that is in the earth beneath, or that is in the waters beneath the earth:**

**[9]Thou shalt not bow down thyself unto them, nor serve them: for I the LORD thy God am a jealous God, visiting the iniquity of the fathers upon the children unto the third and fourth generation of them that hate me,**

[10]And shewing mercy unto thousands of them that love me and keep my commandments.

[11]Thou shalt not take the name of the LORD thy God in vain: for the LORD will not hold him guiltless that taketh his name in vain.

[12]Keep the sabbath day to sanctify it, as the LORD thy God hath commanded thee.

[13]Six days thou shalt labour, and do all thy work:

[14]But the seventh day is the sabbath of the LORD thy God: in it thou shalt not do any work, thou, nor thy son, nor thy daughter, nor thy manservant, nor thy maidservant, nor thine ox, nor thine ass, nor any of thy cattle, nor thy stranger that is within thy gates; that thy manservant and thy maidservant may rest as well as thou.

[15]And remember that thou wast a servant in the land of Egypt, and that the LORD thy God brought thee out thence through a mighty hand and by a stretched out arm: therefore the LORD thy God commanded thee to keep the sabbath day.

[16]Honour thy father and thy mother, as the LORD thy God hath commanded thee; that thy days may be prolonged, and that it may go well with thee, in the land which the LORD thy God giveth thee.

[17]Thou shalt not kill.

[18]Neither shalt thou commit adultery.

[19]Neither shalt thou steal.

[20]Neither shalt thou bear false witness against thy neighbour.

[21]Neither shalt thou desire thy neighbour's wife, neither shalt thou covet thy neighbour's house, his field, or his manservant, or his maidservant, his

**ox, or his ass, or any thing that is thy neighbour's.
(Deuteronomy 5:6-21 KJV)**

These two versions basically mirror each other though the Deuteronomy version is a greater elaboration of the original version. Theological and secular scholars argue that the differences in the 10 Commandment versions, imply a difference in meaning to a commandment or extrapolation of a commandment. As a student of the Exodus version of the 10 Commandments, I immediately recognized a variance in the 4th Commandment in Deuteronomy. In the Exodus version, the commandment starts with the word "Remember" whereas, in the Deuteronomy the verse begins with "Keep". When God told Moses to "Remember" one has to believe that, first, God was giving direct instruction and second, the commandment was in effect before this instruction. I read this and believe that the commandments were in place from creation.

**²And on the seventh day God ended His work which He had done, and He rested on the seventh day from all His work which He had done.**

**³Then God blessed the seventh day and sanctified it, because in it He rested from all His work which God had created and made. (Genesis 2:2-3 NKJV)**

To read the word "Keep", in the Deuteronomy leads me to believe Moses was interpreting the commandment.

This is just one example. I believe the original Exodus version is of divine revelation where the Deuteronomy version was inspired by God and expressed through the intellect of Moses.

Furthermore, an analysis of the 10th Commandment encourages scholarly engagement regarding Exodus's "Thou shall not covet" and Deuteronomy's "Neither thou shall desire". I suspect that the prohibitions are different and could be debated as to how much.

This brings us to the other commandments that Moses address in Deuteronomy. Were these proclamations pertinent to all time?

Apparently so. Jesus clarifies the importance of the Old Testament commands during His "Sermon on the Mount".

> <sup>17</sup>**Think not that I am come to destroy the law, or the prophets: I am not come to destroy, but to fulfil.**
>
> <sup>18</sup>**For verily I say unto you, Till heaven and earth pass, one jot or one tittle shall in no wise pass from the law, till all be fulfilled. (Mathew 5:17-18 KJV)**

To put things into the right perspective, the laws were recorded by Moses and cited by Jesus approximately 1,400 years later. Interestingly enough, most people think the commandments stated in Book of Matthew replaced the 10 Commandments of the Old Testament. Jesus gives two commandants in the Book of Mathew when questioned about the greatest commandments. The Book of Mathew records a conversation between a Pharisee lawyer and Jesus.

> <sup>36</sup>**Master, which is the great commandment in the law?**
>
> <sup>37</sup>**Jesus said unto him, Thou shalt love the Lord thy God with all thy heart, and with all thy soul, and with all thy mind.**
>
> <sup>38</sup>**This is the first and great commandment.**
>
> <sup>39</sup>**And the second is like unto it, Thou shalt love thy neighbour as thyself. (Mathew 22:36-39 KJV)**

Many people believe that this conversation is proof that Jesus replaced the 10 Commandments in the Old Testament with a new commandment. The fact is, Jesus was just quoting what God revealed to Moses. Moses stated this first commandment in Deuteronomy.

> <sup>4</sup>**Hear, O Israel: The LORD our God is one LORD:**
>
> <sup>5</sup>**And thou shalt love the LORD thy God with all thine heart, and with all thy soul, and with all thy might. (Deuteronomy 6:4-5 KJV)**

The second commandment discussed between the Pharisee lawyer and Jesus was again Jesus quoting God's revelation to Moses.

**¹⁸Thou shalt not avenge, nor bear any grudge against the children of thy people, but thou shalt love thy neighbour as thyself: I am the LORD. (Leviticus 19:18 KJV)**

Jesus did not change the law He affirmed the law. These commands given by Jesus are a summary of the ten commandments given to Mankind by God.

After the Apostolic Period, the Catholic Church began a divergence from the Jewish beliefs and traditions. Over 400 years from the time of the first Pope, Peter, the Catholic Church no longer was a branch of Judaism.

In the 5ᵗʰ Century C.E. Saint Augustine of Hippo, Doctor of the Catholic Church, presented the 10 Commandments to the church for catechetical acceptance. It is the official version that is used today in the Catholic Church. Let there be no misunderstanding, the Catholic Church is not just another denomination of Christianity. It is very different from any Protestant denominations.

Though similar to the Mosaic version penned by God Himself, there are distinct differences that deserve comment.

| PROTESTANT | CATHOLIC |
|---|---|
| (Mosaic Law) | (Catechetical Tradition) |

**I** And God spake all these words, saying,

I am the LORD thy God, which have brought thee out of the land of Egypt, out of the house of bondage.

Thou shalt have no other gods before me.

**I** I am the Lord you God: You shall not have strange Gods before me.

**II** Thou shalt not make unto thee any graven image, or any likeness of any thing that is in heaven above, or that is in the earth beneath, or that is in the water under the earth.

Thou shalt not bow down thyself to them, nor serve them: for I the Lord thy God am a jealous God, visiting the iniquity of the fathers upon the children unto the third and fourth generation of them that hate me;

And shewing mercy unto thousands of them that love me, and keep my commandments.

**II** You shall not take the name of the Lord your God in vain.

**III** Thou shalt not take the name of the Lord thy God in vain; for the Lord will not hold him guiltless that taketh his name in vain.

**III** Remember to keep holy the Lord's Day.

**IV** Remember the sabbath day, to keep it holy. Six days shalt thou labour, and do all thy work: But the seventh day is the sabbath of the LORD thy God: in it thou shalt not do any work, thou, nor thy son, nor thy daughter, thy manservant, nor thy maidservant, nor thy cattle, nor thy stranger that is within thy gates: For in six days the LORD made heaven and earth, the sea, and all that in them is, and rested the seventh day: wherefore the LORD blessed the sabbath day, and hallowed it.

**V** Honour thy father and thy mother: that thy days may be long upon the land which the LORD thy God giveth thee.

**VI** Thou shalt not kill.

**VII** Thou shall not commit adultery.

**VIII** Thou shall not steal.

**IX** Thou shalt not bear false witness against thy neighbour.

**X** Thou shalt not covet thy neighbour's house, thou shalt not covet thy neighbour's wife, nor his manservant, nor his maidservant, nor his ox, nor his ass, nor any thing that is thy neighbour's.

**IV** Honor your father and mother.

**V** You shall not kill.

**VI** Thou shall not commit adultery.

**VII** Thou shall not steal.

**VIII** Thou shall not bear false witness against your neighbor.

**IX** Thou shall not covet your neighbor's wife.

**X** Thou shall not covet your neighbor's goods.

The Catholic version of the 10 Commandment is essentially the same as the Protestant version. The main difference is the absence of the Mosaic 2nd Commandment. Some argue that this absence allows Catholicism condonement of idol worship. The Catholic Church sees this commandment as an extension of the 1st Commandment. They believe that if one follows the 1st Commandment they will not create false idols or worship them. Therefore, the church was eliminating a redundancy. To make up for the absence of the 2nd Commandment, the 10th Commandment is split into two parts. The 9th Commandment addresses coveting "thy neighbor's wife". The 10th Commandment addresses coveting "thy neighbor's goods".

# THE 10 COMMANDMENTS

Before we begin our study of the 10 Commandments let us remember what our Lord, Jesus Christ said about the Word of God.

> **⁴But he answered and said, It is written, Man shall not live by bread alone, but by every word that proceedeth out of the mouth of God. (Matthew 4:4 KJV)**

We cannot have eternal life without living by the Word of God. We can never forget this. We must take heed to everything that is written in the Bible because it is the Word of God. The Apostle Paul explains the significance of the Word of God in his second letter to his disciple Timothy.

**<sup>16</sup>Scripture is inspired by God and is profitable for teaching, for reproof, for correction, and for instruction in righteousness,**

**<sup>17</sup>that the man of God may be complete, thoroughly equipped for every good work. (II Timothy 3:16-17 MEV)**

There are those who think that they are good people, and they may be. They may think that by being good, God will give them favor. Their church may even support this ideology, but the reality is, being good will not give you access to eternal life. Jesus explains clearly that keeping God's commandments is imperative for life.

**<sup>17</sup>And he said unto him, Why callest thou me good? there is none good but one, that is, God: but if thou wilt enter into life, keep the commandments. (Matthew 19:17 KJV)**

When contemplating the 10 Commandment, it should not be considered as a whole, but as two themes with a bridging verse. The first 4 commandments are edicts pertaining to the worship of God. The 5<sup>th</sup> commandment is a verse of promise. The last 5 commandments refer to the obligations to our fellow man. The 10 Commandments are a summary of the 613 Old Testament law. They are a covenant between the people of Israel and God.

The application of the greatest commandment and the second commandment as stated by Jesus is such:

- The first four commandments teach us how to love God. If we love God, we will not worship other gods, worship idols or disparage his name and we will remember the Sabbath.

- The next six commandments teach us how to love each other. If we love our neighbor as ourself, we will love our parents, we will not murder, nor covet or have sex out of wedlock, or steal or lie.

These are the basic laws that God commanded the people of Israel to obey. The laws are timeless and have been applicable over the last 2,500 years. These laws were given to understand what God requires of Man to improve their relationship. It teaches us respect for our parents. It also articulates succinctly how we should interact with each other, in our community or wherever we are in the world.

Yes, the 10 Commandments are perfect in providing a standard for righteous and moral living. It is easily understood by anyone who wants to build a relationship with God. Yet there is more profound significance in these commandments, reaching out to us as we meditate on these words.

A person who truly understands the meaning of the 10 Commandments has a different outlook on life. No longer are the commandments viewed as prohibitions that must be obeyed. They become guidelines that we choose to obey. Living by the Law no longer is a burden but lightens our burdens as we navigate the trials of daily living. The 10 Commandments provide the solution to any decision that needs to be made regarding what is good and what is sin.

I encourage everyone to take a moment to look at their lives. Reflect on your anxiety, stress, guilt, desires, relationships and all the other ways of this worldly existence that block the peace of God. Then consider how free you would be if you lived by the commandments given to Moses by our loving God.

God gives us the 10 Commandments with an intended good. They are not rituals contrived by man but are the Words of God written by his hand.

**18And he gave unto Moses, when he had made an end of communing with him upon mount Sinai, two tables of testimony, tables of stone, written with the finger of God. (Exodus 31:18 KJV)**

The 10 commandments are the foundation of God's covenant with his people. God first spoke these commandments to Moses, then God wrote them on two stone tablets to be stored in the Ark of the Covenant for the people to always have.

> **[13]He declared to you his covenant, the Ten Commandments, which he commanded you to follow and then wrote them on two stone tablets. (Deuteronomy 4:13 NKJV)**

These commandments are a blessing and benefit for all Man. On a personal level as well as a societal level, abiding by these commandments will provide stability and peace and a greater understanding of the will of God.

# THEME 1:

# Our Duties To God

King Solomon was the wisest man ever on Earth. He understood what was Mans obligation to the Lord. He was a great teacher and wanted to impart his knowledge to the people of Israel. First and foremost, he wanted people to understand their duty to God.

> **13Now all has been heard; here is the conclusion of the matter: Fear God and keep his commandments, for this is the duty of all mankind.**
>
> **14For God will bring every deed into judgment, including every hidden thing, whether it is good or evil. (Ecclesiastes 12:13-14 NIV)**

God begins the commandments with a theme of obedience in order to create a strong bond. His desire to have a strong bond with us is a holy mystery to be gratefully acknowledged, not deciphered. We should love God because of His promises to those who obey Him. If for no other reason, we should love God because He is our source of life now in this life and in the next.

The Old Testament makes it clear that the 10 Commandments are special apodictic laws separate from the other 603 conventional Laws of Moses. With the sacrifice of Jesus on the cross, unity of the Laws of God and the conventional Laws of Moses were established.

> **15by setting aside in his flesh the law with its commands and regulations. His purpose was to create in himself one new humanity out of the two, thus making peace, (Ephesians 2:15 NIV)**

King Solomon tells us that we are happy when we keep the law (Proverbs 29:18). Instead of the lawlessness that follows the selfish desires for worldly things, prosperity and happiness is the reward for obeying God's commandments.

# COMMANDMENT I

**²I am the LORD thy God, which have brought thee out of the land of Egypt, out of the house of bondage.**

**³Thou shalt have no other gods before me. (Mathew 20:2-3 KJV)**

The Lord starts this commandment with a statement of existence and a statement of execution. He emphatically declares who He is. This declaration exposes the impotence of all the man-made gods of Egypt and the rest of the world. In this commandment, God reminds the people of Israel of the miracles performed in Egypt. It is a reminder of the miracles executed on the way to Mount Sinai from the parting of the Red Sea, the provision of food and water, the preservation of their clothing and shoes, protection from the unbearable heat during the day and the cold at night, and the first mention of the importance of the importance of the Sabbath. This commandment tells us, by fiat, God created the heavens and the Earth and is the ultimate power of the Universe. He is the supreme guiding influence over our lives. Everything that we have and all that we are is from Him.

Now that God has established Himself as the All-mighty, He gives us His first and most important command of obedience, "Thou shalt have no other gods before me". God does not allow a provision for any other gods. His statement is adamant. It is a command not a suggestion. It is said with such force, the power of consequence can be felt from the pages of the Bible itself.

Let us first look at this statement for more clarity. Superficially, one would read this command and say this doesn't apply to them because they believe in God. This casual reflection misses the complete message of the commandment. Of course, the command is to accept the God of Abraham, the God of Jacob, the God of Moses, as the true living God, by faith and without doubt. But what of the other gods? What about Baal, Shiva, Odin, Ra, Zeus, Isis, Osiris or any of the thousands of other gods people worship? It is easy to think of these imaginations and say, "I would never worship any of these gods".

What is frequently unnoticed, is that God is not only talking about religious figures. Numerous entities are substituted for God daily without the offender even being aware they are sinning. Things like money, possessions, status, power and even science frequently are not considered as substitutes for God, but multitudes worship these distractions to the detriment of their soul. These people may or may not go to church but have some awareness that God is supposed to be the supreme being and creator of the universe.

The ones who go to church and are taking their religion for granted are performing ritual and tradition. Their faith is not in God. They may just as well not go to church. Their faith is a false religion or false god based on inventions of Man. The time that is devoted to their false god(s) detract from worship of the true God. The perfect example is with regard to money. People have focused all their energy and time in an attempt to attain more and more of it. People worship money. It is safe to say their adoration leans toward their greed and lust which are sins and of Satan. The Apostle Paul explains this predicament.

**¹⁶Do you not know that to whom you yield yourselves as slaves to obey, you are slaves of the one whom you obey, whether of sin leading to death, or of obedience leading to righteousness? (Romans 6:16 MEV)**

God is clear on what He wants. There is no middle ground. Either you choose to adhere to the commandment or serve and obey your own lust. In the end, greed and lust aren't fulfilling and cannot do anything positive towards your relationship with God. If it is Gods will for you to be prosperous, He will provide.

> **⁸This book of the law shall not depart out of thy mouth; but thou shalt meditate therein day and night, that thou mayest observe to do according to all that is written therein: for then thou shalt make thy way prosperous, and then thou shalt have good success. (Joshua 1:8 KJV)**

Those who do not go to church or maybe not even believe in God should consider these words. Where they say they serve God, they acquiesce to worship things of the world. Jesus says:

> **²⁴No man can serve two masters: for either he will hate the one and love the other; or else he will hold to the one and despise the other. Ye cannot serve God and mammon. (Matthew 6:24 KJV)**

Consider this example of the Pharisees and Sadducees. For the most part these proclaimed holy, pious men were the most guilty of equivocality. Their public persona exhibited their commitment to their belief in God, with displays of praying loudly on the steps of the synagogue for all to see. They displayed their pride in their knowledge of the Laws of Moses and claimed Jesus to be blasphemous. This may have been impressive to the many people of Israel but not to God. God knew their hearts. He knew that their ulterior motive was power, status and money and their need to acquire and retain them. For these reasons, they hated the increasing influence of Jesus and plotted to kill Him. The Pharisees and Sadducee did not serve God, they served worldly things.

In the 1ˢᵗ Commandment, God establishes himself as the definitive authority in the Universe. No man-made god can come close to His omnipotence. He chose the people of Israel to be His chosen people and instituted monotheism. The proximate civilizations, Egyptians, Hittites, Mesopotamians, Canaanites and Amorites were not favored by God and created their own gods according to polytheistic tradition, to which God unambiguously forbade.

But God wants us to meditate on the deeper wisdom of this commandment. He wants us to recognize what is the real focus of our worship. The prophet Malachi wants us to be clear about who to worship. He wants us to think about what will lead us to life and what will lead us to death as he prophesizes about the coming of the Messiah.

> [18]And you will again see the distinction between the righteous and the wicked, between those who serve God and those who do not. (Malachi 3:18 NIV)

We must always understand that living in this world is temporary. God has granted us 120 years to prove our devotion to Him. In exchange, He will grant us eternal life. The concept can be challenging to understand, this concept of eternal life. It is truly a mystery of God.

Understandably, it is difficult living in this world. To survive is to endure trials throughout life. This is the same for the Christian and the non-believer. God wants us to prosper but not at the cost of replacing Him with an object of the world. He wants us to never direct our worship toward anything that He has created or regard it as the source of our life and blessings. Only God deserves the recognition and never anything He has created. The Apostle John gives us sagacious advice regarding the things of this world.

> [15]Love not the world, neither the things that are in the world. If any man loves the world, the love of the Father is not in him. (1 John 2:15 KJV)

# COMMANDMENT II

The 2nd Commandment is closely linked to the 1st Commandment which commands us not to have any other gods. To have other gods is idolatrous. During the time of Moses, the people of Israel were surrounded by nations that were polytheistic and worshiped many gods. These gods were carved or shaped in the form of animals, insects or humanoids. It was very common to sacrifice to these images as well as performing other acts of worship. In this commandment, God strictly forbids any association with these pagan practices. Many nations today have carved gods and goddesses which are obvious violation of this commandment.

Even many Christian religions have representations of Jesus and the virgin Mary as sources of worship.

But not all idolatrous practice is related to religious activity. Idols can be anything that one seeks to find identity and security other than God. This can be observed in the love and worship of money, substance addiction (alcohol, tobacco, illegal drugs) sex, power, possessions. Idolatry can also be subtle and many not even be recognized. In attempts to honor God we sometimes put our works above God. Our commitments to hobbies, sports, entertainment, employment, charity work and even family can replace one's relationship with God and become the object of our worship. Whether idolatrous ideology is obvious or subtle, whenever one feels validated by their actions or works, they are breaking the 2nd Commandment. Idolatry is not the answer to satisfy one's contentment. It will never fulfill the heart with peace and self-actualization. Only God can give one this fulfillment. Idolatry only distracts from God and give cause for His anger. He tells us that He is a "jealous God" and makes idolatry a sin. Therefore, we must be careful not to allow worldly things to become the objects of our worship. This the Lord, our God abhors.

The 2nd Commandment says,

> **4Thou shalt not make unto thee any graven image, or any likeness of any thing that is in heaven above, or that is in the earth beneath, or that is in the water under the earth.**
>
> **5Thou shalt not bow down thyself to them, nor serve them: for I the LORD thy God am a jealous God, visiting the iniquity of the fathers upon the children unto the third and fourth generation of them that hate me;**
>
> **6And shewing mercy unto thousands of them that love me and keep my commandments. (Exodus 4-6 KJV)**

God first gave us an impression of likeness in the Book of Genesis. He states that Man is created in His likeness, but this was only a clue.

> **26And God said, Let us make man in our image, after our likeness: and let them have dominion over the fish of the sea, and over the fowl of the air,**

and over the cattle, and over all the earth, and over every creeping thing that creepeth upon the earth.

²⁷So God created man in his own image, in the image of God created he him; male and female created he them. (Genesis 1:26-27 KJV)

God never describes what He looks like, in fact, he was resolute in concealing his appearance. God is the embodiment of purity and Man being corruptible cannot see His face and live.

²⁰And he said, Thou canst not see my face: for there shall no man see me, and live.

²¹And the LORD said, Behold, there is a place by me, and thou shalt stand upon a rock:

²²And it shall come to pass, while my glory passeth by, that I will put thee in a clift of the rock, and will cover thee with my hand while I pass by:

²³And I will take away mine hand, and thou shalt see my back parts: but my face shall not be seen. (Exodus 33:20-23 KJV)

**Images of God**

God was speaking to Moses in the previous verses. It is assumed Moses spoke to God face-to-face, but this is never so. Even in these verses God said Moses would only see His "back parts". Though God explains in Genesis that we are made in His likeness we cannot assume that his "back parts" are like ours. We can't assume his face is like ours. Therefore, we can't assume that his definition of "likeness" is the same as ours.

In this commandment, God specifically tells us to not try and figure out what He looks like. We are too immoral and imperfect to gaze upon His presence and live. Any representation we create of Him would be inaccurate and is idolatrous.

Making an image of God is impossible. He is not corporeal, but is a spiritual essence. Therefore, he is invisible. He was never seen by anyone according to the Bible, so there is no reference as to what he should look like. Generally, no artist makes a serious attempt at drawing or painting God. *Quod invisibile est, pingi non potest* [There is no depicting the invisible, Saint Ambrose of Milan].

**Images of Jesus**

On the other hand, there are many interpretations of Jesus and what he looks likes. What do we really know about Jesus? We know He was of Jewish descent born in Bethlehem, a city in the central West Bank of Palestine, 6.2 miles southwest of Jerusalem.

Jesus was described as being average, which means He was probably a little over 5 feet tall. He would have had Mediterranean skin tones, dark hair and probably a full beard, as was tradition. He was a carpenter by trade, so He was probably moderately muscular. However, nowhere in the New Testament are His facial features described.

Since no one has seen the face of God, artist have turned to His son, Jesus as the representative of divinity. Jesus is part of the trinity and is therefore God. People have used images and painting of Jesus to pray to and worship ever since the paintings started to appear.

Initially, Christians were in hiding from persecution by the Romans for the first three centuries. They identified each other by casually drawing the sign of the fish, ichthus, in the dirt. The symbolism was analogous to the quote from Jesus, "I will make you fishers of men". Jesus wanted his disciples and all Christians to spread His gospel.

Ichthus was used until the mid-third century as the symbol of Christianity. Around this time images of Jesus started to emerge. These images became paintings and were even carried with priest to show the people what they determined Jesus looked like. The problem with the paintings lies in the fact that Jesus had been dead for approximately 300 years, and no one knew what He looked like.

The oldest representation of Jesus is a painting found on the wall in the baptismal chamber in the Dura-Europos church in Syria. It is titled "The Healing of the Paralytic" and depicts the famous story in the Gospel of Luke of Jesus healing a paralyzed man who was lowered from a hole in the ceiling by his friends to get an audience with Jesus. Jesus heals the man and tells him to get up, carry his bed and walk. This painting dates back to approximately 235 C.E. In this painting the image of Jesus is little more than a caricature.

The earliest painting of Jesus as a person was found in the Catacomb of San Callisto, Rome, Italy. This painting is called "The Good Shepherd". In this painting, a young beardless Jesus is seen with a lamb draped around His shoulders leading other sheep. Christianity embraces the interpretation of this image to represent Jesus, the caretaker of His flock or church. The painting is dated to the mid-3rd Century, some 300 years after his death. This image is a common image amongst Greek art, especially sculpture and seen throughout Greece and Italy. This image was not a representation of anyone in particular. Its features were general and nondescript.

Today there are hundreds, thousands of paintings of Jesus. There are ethnic paintings of Jesus. There are sport figure paintings, comedic paintings, businessmen paintings, and even blasphemous pornographic paintings. It doesn't stop with Jesus; some artists have endeavored to paint God. This blasphemy happens in the face of no information or references to what God or Jesus look like.

I don't know what Jesus looks like, but I do know that He did not look like the Caucasian created by Western Christians. Jesus was Jewish, born and raised in the Middle East. It only makes sense that Jesus would look like all other Middle Easterners, dark skin with Mediterranean undertones. So how did He become Caucasian (white)?

When the Roman Emperor Constantine converted to Christianity and declared it the state religion, Jesus became popular. As Jesus's popularity grew more images of Him started to appear. The classic representation of Jesus as a white man with brown hair, a beard, and a halo became prolific under Emperor Constantine and most of the art coming out of Rome and was commissioned by either the Emperor or Catholic Church. Artist painted images of Jesus to look more like them with European features rather than Jewish features because Jews were marginalized by Romans, Greeks and other non-Jewish factions in the imperial cities. By the 6th Century C.E., Byzantine artist portrayed Jesus as having white skin, a beard, with slightly wavy to straight hair parted in the middle. Dr. Christena Cleveland of the Duke Divinity School tells us that earlier depictions of Jesus, i.e. 300 C.E., showed Him with darker complexion.

By the 13th Century C.E. (Middle Ages), the white Jesus was cemented in the Roman Empire. However, papal authority would now define Christianity and images of Christianity. The Pope could not have the populace believe that Jesus was not white, in lieu of the fact that Jesus was Jewish. The Catholic Church misinterprets the Bible by associating the whiteness of Jesus's skin with the color white being symbolic for purity, Jesus being the 'lamb of God' and the Holy Spirit depicted as a white dove. This association does not mean that Jesus is white. In fact, this association has been misused to justify racism and slavery.

1st Century C.E. letters were discovered that identified what Jesus looked like. The most famous letter was from one Pulbius Lentulus (circa 14-37 C.E.) delivered to the Roman Senate. This letter describes Jesus as being tall with wavy hair, rosey cheeks and blue eyes. This supported the Pope's position and the Catholic Church validated this letter and established this identity as factual. This letter was later found to be fraudulent.

Part of the issues with Muslims and Christians during the 'Holy Wars' was this depiction of Jesus. The Muslims portrayed Jesus as dark complected while Christians portrayed Jesus as white. It was essential for the Christians to embrace the whiteness of Jesus as non-believers were non-white. Most of the Christian forces were Crusaders from Europe and could not except a non-white Messiah.

In the 19th Century C.E., Hitler and the Nazi idealist invented a concept of 'Positive Christianity'. This ideology posited an Aryan Jesus of Nordic descent. This made Jesus even paler and whiter. The Nazi scholars presented theories that Galilee was a non-Jewish region speaking an Indo-European language. Religious Judaism is separate from ethnic or racial Judaism. The Nazi's belief in Positive Christianity was the justification for their anti-sematic racism. Every modern scholar debunks the Nazi ideology.

Even now, in the 20th Century C.E., white actors have been cast as Jesus in over twenty films about Christ. The first film about Jesus with a Middle Eastern actor debuted in 2015 C.E. Though the arguments regarding his skin color may be shifting the scales of his nationality, no one knows what he actually looked like. Every image that is seen of Him, of which there are millions, is idolatrous misrepresentations not to be prayed to.

## Idols

God emphatically commands us not to create images of Him. It could not be any clearer in the beginning of this commandment. Creation of any idols as gods is as damnable. To worship an idol clearly excludes God as our Heavenly Father and spiritual presence.

Ultimately, idolatry is a sin of the heart. We create idols to ease the needs of love, security, worth, significance, confidence, et cetera. The idol is something tangible that grounds the idolater to a perceived real presence. When one looks for security in something besides God, they have given up on their faith in God and create their own deity to solve their problems This is an effort in futility.

Idols can do nothing to cause change or effect miracles as evidenced by the gods of Egypt.

The same principles apply when our worship leads us to worldly pursuits. As noted in the 1st Commandment, false gods are created from our greed and lust. The worship of money, power and status can supersede the simplicity of loving God. And lest we forget, worldly pursuits also include addictions. Addictions may satisfy in the short term but will ultimately leave one empty and unsatisfied.

God promises to punish those who create these idols for generations. He tells us He is jealous. He does not want any distractions to make us waver from our love for Him.

He also promises to reward those who stay faithful and obey His commandments.

# COMMANDMENT III

**⁷Thou shalt not take the name of the LORD thy God in vain; for the LORD will not hold him guiltless that taketh his name in vain. (Exodus 20:7 KJV)**

The Holman Christian Standard Bible reinterprets this verse as,

**⁷Do not misuse the name of the LORD your God, because the LORD will not leave anyone unpunished who misuses His name. (Exodus 20:7 HCSB)**

This Holman Christian Standard Bible interpretation of the 3ʳᵈ Commandment, in my opinion, is a superficial exclamation of the message that God wants conveyed. To only reference the misuse of the Lord's name is only half of the intention. This, however, is what most people think of when or if they think of this commandment.

Taking "the Lord's name" in vain expands to mean a general disrespect towards God. God will not tolerate those who disrespect or show a lack of reverence towards Him. He tells us in this commandment that there is impending punishment for those who chose to ignore this command.

The confusion in the aforementioned biblical verses is in the definition of the word 'vain' from the King James Version and the word 'misuse' interpreted from the Holman Christian Standard Bible. The King James Version translates the English word 'vain' from the Hebrew word 'shav'. This word means worthlessness, vanity, lie, falsehood or nothingness depending on how it is used in sentence. In the King James version of this commandment, vain would suggest that God is worthless.

The Holman Christian Standard Bible is interpreted by a method called Dynamic Equivalence. This method of interpretation attempts to make the material easier to understand. This method doesn't always capture the complete meaning in its interpretation since it uses equivalent terminology instead of actual translation. This doesn't mean its inaccurate but just not from the original Aramaic, Hebrew or Greek text. In replacing 'vain' with misuse, the meaning of the verse suggest that misuse of God's name is a misappropriation of his name for an unintended purpose. While this is partially accurate, the verse makes no reference to reverence, which is the theme of this verse.

**²⁴Only fear the Lord and serve Him in truth with all your heart; for consider what great things He has done for you. (Samuel 12:24 NIV)**

Taking God's name in vain refers to the abuse, misuse, blasphemy, cursing, or manipulation of the Lord's name. So, use of God's name in vain involves:

1.  Trivializing His name by looking at it as being insignificant.

2.  Trying to use it to advance negative purposes (the way priests of false religions used the names of their false gods).

3.  Using it in worship thoughtlessly.

4.  Using profanity or blasphemy is obvious violations of the 3ʳᵈ Commandment. Sometimes people substitute words (euphemisms) for the name of God.

**³¹Therefore shall ye keep my commandments, and do them: I am the LORD.**

**³²Neither shall ye profane my holy name; but I will be hallowed among the children of Israel: I am the LORD which hallow you, (Leviticus 22:31-32 KJV)**

The 3ʳᵈ Commandment is a commandment of reverence. Reverence occurs in our thoughts and in our speech. Contemplating the deeper meaning of this verse unlocks our heart to God's intended purpose and true understanding of this command.

The 3rd Commandment has two parts. The first part is a command for reverence. The second part of this commandment is the consequence for the lack of reverence.

## Reverence in Thought

Respect is the cornerstone of good relationships. The quality of our relationship with God depends on the love and regard we have for Him. It also depends on the way we express respect for Him in the presence of others. We are expected always to honor who and what He is. Reverence is a deeper respect that starts in our heart, is felt in our soul and observed outwardly in our actions. Because God's power and majesty is unsurpassed, He deserves this reverence.

The people of Israel were witness to the power and majesty of God. They witnessed the power over the gods of Egypt and the Pharaoh, Amenhotep II. They experienced His benevolence with provisions of manna and water while in the desert. They witnessed the miracle of the parting of the Red Sea. They observed His presence with a cloud during the day and fire at night when in the desert of Sinai.

God wanted to teach the people of Israel that they needed to be reverent. All the acts he performed in their presence was to prove his omnipotence and His worthiness of reverence. Additionally, He provided 613 laws to Moses to teach the people reverence. These laws relate to purity, holiness and worship. Those of righteous nature recognize and revere their God. Those of sinful nature do not know how to worship a holy God with reverence. They have no respect for what God has done for His people. There rejections will lead to dire eternal consequences. God tells us this in the 3rd Commandment. He knows who obeys Him and who dishonors Him.

With the coming of Jesus, God was now among Man. He preached reverence of God. This would be demonstrated with a willingness to die to self and live by His commands, to accept Jesus as the redeemer of Sins and the conduit to God through faith. Unlike Old Testament edicts to obey the Laws of Moses, salvation is a gift from God as a result of faith and acceptance of Jesus as our Savior.

> [20]I have been crucified with Christ; it is no longer I who live, but Christ lives in me; and the *life* which I now live in the flesh I live by faith in the Son of God, who loved me and gave Himself for me. (Galatians 2:20 NKJV)

In the famous Lord's Prayer in the Book of Matthew, Jesus is asked by His disciples how should they pray. Jesus instructs them to begin their prayers with reverence to God.

> [9]In this manner, therefore, pray:
> Our Father in heaven,
> Hallowed be Your name.
>
> [10]Your kingdom come.
> Your will be done
>
> On earth as *it is* in heaven.
>
> [11]Give us this day our daily bread.
>
> [12]And forgive us our debts,
> As we forgive our debtors.
> [13]And do not lead us into temptation,
>
> But deliver us from the evil one.
> [a] For Yours is the kingdom and the power and the glory forever. Amen. (Matthew 6:9-13 NKJV)

He ends the prayer with reverence. The key word in this prayer is at the beginning. It is the word Hallowed. Hallowed is a special word. It means 'setting apart as Holy'. The Lord is set apart as Holy. The only other hallowed personages are Jesus and the Holy Spirit and as we know they are separate but one.

**<sup>28</sup>Therefore, since we are receiving a kingdom that cannot be shaken, let us be thankful, and so worship God acceptably with reverence and awe, (Hebrews 12:28 NIV)**

## Reverence in Speech

Human nature is evil and wrought with sin. The evil comes from within. It is in our hearts and our minds. We exhibit this by our actions and our words.

The Apostle James tells us the tongue is evil.

**<sup>8</sup>But the tongue can no man tame; it is an unruly evil, full of deadly poison. (James 3:8 KJV)**

Out of our mouths comes all sorts of vile profanities. Specifically, the lack of reverence to His majesty or disrespectful use of the Lord's name in casual conversations. Many people think that taking the Lord's name in vain is only in reference with swearing. Others think that asking God to grant insignificant intentions is another form of using His name in vain.

"God Damn It". When used in condemnation of some evil or satanic exposure, the expletive is appropriate. Unlike "G-d Dammit" which has a thousand different meanings for a thousand different people, the use of the Lord's name in this regard is an absolute disrespect for His majesty and authority. It seems to me that this expletive is used mostly to express frustration.

Using the Lord's name in a flippant, degrading or in any disrespectful manner expresses an attitude of disdaining the relationship we are supposed to have with Him. This can vary from careless disregard to hostility and antagonism. It covers misusing God's name in any way.

The use of His name in vain includes God the Father, God the Son and God the Spirit. Often people will use the Lord's name in casual discourse. Using terms such as O God!, Jesus Christ!, God

Dammit!, O Christ! Or any other way is to use the Lord's name in vain. Many believe that using these expressions are permissible.

The phrase, "Lord's name in vain" has various meanings. As mentioned previously, most think inappropriate use of His name only applies to swearing. Inappropriate use also means to misuse His name in oaths, in inappropriate joking or disparagement of God. How often have you heard the expression, "I swear to God", or the court expression, "I swear to tell the truth, the whole truth, and nothing but the truth, so help me God." "Oh My God" is a commonplace exclamation. Even well intended Christians use this exclamation in substitution of "Wow" not realizing that this too is an irreverent use of His name.

> [31]**Therefore shall ye keep my commandments, and do them: I am the LORD.**
>
> [32]**Neither shall ye profane my holy name; but I will be hallowed among the children of Israel: I am the LORD which hallow you, (Leviticus 22:31-32 KJV)**

Throughout humankind's history, Man has sworn to some greater power. The Greeks would swear by their Zeus, Hera or the god for the specific situation. The Egyptians swore to their gods Isis, Ra, Anubis again to the god for the situation. Swearing to another god violates the 1st, 2nd and 3rd Commandments.

The Apostle James tells us,

> [5]**But above all things, my brethren, swear not, neither by heaven, neither by the earth, neither by any other oath: but let your yea be yea; and your nay, nay; lest ye fall into condemnation. (James 12:5 KJV)**

Swearing in this manner, whether formal or casual, was a declared promise of truth. This practice continues today regardless of the commandment.

To understand why God makes reverence a command, we must try to understand His perspective of His name. The entirety of God's being, especially His glory, are manifested in His name. King David tells us that his name is "holy and awesome". Jesus, in teaching His disciples how to pray, begins the prayer with "Our father, who art in Heaven, hallowed by thy name" (Matthew 6:9). Jesus is telling us that the name of God is to be venerated and foremost in our prayers. We are to remember that God is awe-inspiring and celebrated for his "unfailing love and great compassion" (Psalm 51:1 KJV). This is a statement of allegiance.

The second part of this commandment tells us, "the Lord will not hold him guiltless". The 3ʳᵈ Commandment forbids the irreverent use of the Lord's name as that would be an expression of lack of respect for God Himself. To that end, there are consequences for using His name in vain. God tells us,

**¹²And ye shall not swear by my name falsely, neither shalt thou profane the name of thy God: I am the Lord. (Leviticus 19:12 KJV)**

When people use God's name in vain, they are disrespecting, denying or ignoring His existence. This is mockery. In the Biblical sense, mockery is being hypocritical. One who professes to be reverent to God and uses his name in vain is pretending to love and serve Him. This person is insincere and does not represent the earnestness of the heart. It is a serious offense to God. At some point God will address this disobedience.

**⁷Be not deceived; God is not mocked: for whatsoever a man soweth, that shall he also reap. (Galatians 6:7 KJV)**

The Apostle Paul goes on to explain the consequence of mocking God.

**⁸For he that soweth to his flesh shall of the flesh reap corruption; but he that soweth to the Spirit shall of the Spirit reap life everlasting. (Galatian 6:8 KJV)**

To mock God is to mock all that is holy. God will not hold those guiltless who use His name in vain. This isn't something that you can hide from God. Jesus states, "I know your works".

**¹⁵"I know your works: you are neither cold nor hot. Would that you were either cold or hot!**

**¹⁶So, because you are lukewarm, and neither hot nor cold, I will spit you out of my mouth. (Revelations 3:15-16 KJV)**

He knows who soweth righteousness or who soweth mockery. Those who choose to ignore the 3ʳᵈ Commandment are putting their salvation in jeopardy. This is the inevitable consequence of not being mindful of the Lord's holiness, of being a hypocrite. God's name has power. It must never be taken for granted.

The disregard for the Lord's name in one's mouths show that Satan is in their hearts. Our belief starts in our hearts. If the heart is good, the mind and faith follow. God calls for the heart.

**²⁶My son, give me your heart, and let your eyes observe my ways. (Proverbs 23:26 MEV)**

When one uses His name in vain, they are disavowing their love for God. With repetition it becomes easier and easier to disrespect God. As this commandment is discounted, Satan makes greater inroads into their heart, increasing doubt in the commitment to the other commandments.

In the Old Testament, Moses and the other prophets told the people to demonstrate reverence to God by the way we live. In order to live righteously, we must endeavor to understand God's nature and make it our life's work to worship Him. This requires one to reject ungodliness and worldly things. This also requires one to show reverence by living by the Laws of God.

# COMMANDMENT IV

**⁸Remember the sabbath day, to keep it holy.**

**⁹Six days shalt thou labour, and do all thy work:**

**¹⁰But the seventh day is the sabbath of the LORD thy God: in it thou shalt not do any work, thou, nor thy son, nor thy daughter, thy manservant, nor thy maidservant, nor thy cattle, nor thy stranger that is within thy gates:**

**¹¹For in six days the LORD made heaven and earth, the sea, and all that in them is, and rested the seventh day: wherefore the LORD blessed the sabbath day, and hallowed it. (Exodus 20:8-11 KJV)**

The 4th Commandment is the last of the commandments the Lord requires of Man to build the appropriate relationship with Him. It is an important commandment that is a direct conflict between the Sabbath and the majoritive Christian tradition of Sunday worship. Sunday worship, which started in 321 C.E. (Schaff, 1884) has flourished unchallenged by most modern Christian denominations. It is convenient for modern society since it doesn't disrupt the flow of the weekend for Christians and non-Christians alike. Most people don't even give thought to the Sabbath. The Pew Research Center found that just three-in-ten U.S. adults know that the Jewish Sabbath begins on Friday. Sabbath is generally viewed as an antiquated commandment that does not conform to nuances of modern society.

The 4th Commandment begins with the word "Remember". This is most important as this commandment comes to us from the beginning of creation. In Genesis, the Lord took 6 days to create the Heavens and the Earth. On the 6th day He created Man. On the 7th day He rested, creating the Sabbath Day. This was approximately 2,500 years before God gave this commandment to Moses.

> [31]**And God saw every thing that he had made, and, behold, it was very good. And the evening and the morning were the sixth day. (Genesis 1:31 KJV)**
>
> [2]**And on the seventh day God ended his work which he had made; and he rested on the seventh day from all his work which he had made.**
>
> [3]**And God blessed the seventh day, and sanctified it: because that in it he had rested from all his work which God created and made. (Genesis 2:2-3 KJV)**

Think about the significance of this day. This was the first 7th day of time, which He honored and established His greatest honor on this day for all time. The first to honor this day was God Himself. He rested and blessed this day and made this day Holy. The Sabbath is a memorial to God, the Creator.

God made this day for Man. He is the one to give it its name. At that time, He explained the concept of Sanctification (set aside for sacred use) to Adam and Eve as they were the only humans on the 7th day of creation. (Andrews, 1998) This Sanctification was put into existence to last for all time.

> [14]**I know that, whatsoever God doeth, it shall be for ever: nothing can be put to it, nor any thing taken from it: and God doeth it, that men should fear before him. (Ecclesiastes 3:14 KJV)**

The authority of the 4th Commandment is based upon the original decree of God making it hallowed. Since Adam and Eve were the first of the human family, God was imposing the substance of this commandment on them as the representatives of Mankind.

It was important to God for humans to understand who their Creator is. He wants us to remember that at the end of the first week of existence, He rested and made the 7th day holy. In turn, He wants Man to follow His example and keep that day holy also and make it a day of worship and relationship building with Him.

## WHAT IS THE SABBATH CONTROVERSY?

Before addressing what the Lord expects of us on the Sabbath, an explanation of the how Sunday became the official day of worship in the majority of the Christian world is in order. Thousands of Christian denominations will have reasoned explanations on how they can justify the change of Sabbath to Sunday. Meanwhile, there are 500 denominations and 100 languages internationally that continue to worship on the Biblical Sabbath.

To begin with, clarity of terminology is necessary.

The seven-day cycle and the original names of the days of the week were first introduced by the Babylonians of ancient Mesopotamia over 3,000 years ago. Babylonian astrologers believed that human life was manipulated by seven celestial bodies, which they saw as moving around a stationary Earth. They had a 24-hour day and a monthly cycle. For simplicity's sake, the Babylonians needed a time unit measurement that was longer than day but shorter than a month. Their month revolved around the lunar cycle. Similar to our calendar, the lunar cycle lasts approximately 29 and a half days. The Babylonians established the 7-day week to approximate the lunar cycle. They used Sunday as the first day of the week. It is believed that the names were given after the celestial bodies they could see, Sun, Moon, Mercury, Venus, Mars, Saturn, Jupiter (Falk, 1999).

**Sunday**: Shamash - The god of law and justice. The Sun

**Monday**: Sin – The god of the Moon. The Moon

**Tuesday**: Nergal – The god of death and plague. The planet Mars

**Wednesday**: Nabu – The god of knowledge, wisdom, writing and messengers. The planet Mercury

**Thursday**: Marduk – The national god of the Babylonians. The planet Jupiter

**Friday**: Istar – the goddess of love, beauty, sex, war, violence and political power. The planet Venus

**Saturday**: Saturn – The eldest of the gods. The planet Saturn

As the Greek general Alexander the Great conquered more of the Middle East, the belief systems of the Middle East started to penetrate Mediterranean. The Romans and Greeks adopted the Babylonian tradition but installed their gods as the names of the days. This occurred with the inauguration of the Julian Calendar in the 1st Century B.C.E.

Prior to this the Romans used an 8-day work week to tract time. This was called the "nundinal cycle", a market cycle of 8 days labeled with the letters A through H where 7 days were devoted to work but the 8th day was time away from work to allow citizens to shop for the upcoming week. People from outside the city would also come to the city for this "market day". This was a specific time for commerce. This 8-day work week fell out of favor with introduction of the Julian calendar.

- **Sunday:** dies Solis, "day of the Sun" It was symbolized with a halo behind the head and represented worship of the Sun

- **Monday:** dies Lunae, "day of the Moon"

- **Tuesday:** dies Martis, "day of Mars" (Roman god of war)

- **Wednesday:** dies Mercurii, "day of Mercury" (Roman messenger of the gods and god of commerce, travel, thievery, eloquence, and science.)

- **Thursday:** dies Iovis, "day of Jupiter" (Roman god who created thunder and lightning, patron of the Roman state)

- **Friday:** dies Veneris, "day of Venus" (Roman goddess of love and beauty)

- **Saturday:** dies Saturni, "day of Saturn" (Roman god of agriculture)

During the fall of the Western Roman Empire, the Germanic people incorporated the Roman week replacing the weekdays with their deities in a process known as *interpretatio germanica* (Grimm, 2004). This occurred after 200 C.E. but no later than 600 C.E. and before Christian introduction into Germania. The only change from the Babylonian week was the replacement of the names with local gods. The system grew in popularity, and in 321 C.E. the "week" was officially recognized by the Roman emperor Constantine the Great in Rome. Constantine was a Mithras sun cult worshiper. He decreed that Sunday would be observed as the Roman's official day of rest and sanctioned Christians to worship only on this day, declaring: "On the venerable Day of the Sun let the magistrates and people residing in cities rest and let all workshops be closed in the country." (Christian Forum, 2018) More on this later.

When the Anglo-Saxons invaded Great Britain, they adopted the Roman-Greco week and like the Romans and Greeks, the Anglo-Saxons replaced the names with their own deities. They did not change Saturday though.

- **Sunday:** Sunnandæg, Sun's Day. The Sun gave people light and warmth every day. They decided to name the first (or last) day of the week after the Sun.

- **Monday:** Mōnandæg, Moon's Day. The Moon was thought to be very important in the lives of people and their crops.

- **Tuesday:** Tīwesdæg, Tiw's Day. Tiw, or Tyr, was a Norse god known for his sense of justice.

- **Wednesday:** Wōdnesdæg, Woden's Day. Woden, or Odin, was a Norse god who was one of the most powerful of them all.

- **Thursday:** Þunresdæg, Thor's Day. Thor was a Norse god who wielded a giant hammer. He was the god of thunder.

- **Friday**: Frīgedæg, Frigg's Day. Frigg was a Norse god equal in power to Odin. She wqs the queen of the Norse gods.

- **Saturday**: Sæternesdæg, Seater's Day or Saturn's Day. Saturn was a Roman god.

The English adopted these pagan names and are the same names (with minor variation) we use today.

The Babylonians established Sunday as the first day of the week. Traditionally within the Judeo-Christian tradition, the first day of the week has always been the Sunday. The Romans, the Greeks, the Visigoths (people of Germania), the Anglo-Saxons and English continued this tradition, as do the rest of Western Civilization. Most importantly, God establishes a 7-day week with Sunday being the 1st day and Saturday being the 7th day.

## The Controversy

Rome was the religious capital of the Roman Empire and was by majority pagan. The predominant pagan religious practiced their day of rest and worship on Sunday. However, this only became important to the Romans during the later periods of Roman history. The Romans did not see the sun as a god, they actually worshiped the sun. The main holiday of the sun worshipers was the feast of the Sol Invictus (Unconquered Sun). This was traditionally celebrated on December 25th. This was the shortest day of the year and herald the coming of the lengthy days of Sun. December 25th was established by the Julian Calendar. The Catholic Church used this holiday to their advantage and eventually replaced the holiday with the Christian Christmas as the celebration of the birth of Jesus Christ. Using the same day, the Catholic Church captured the pagan and Christian audience.

The 1st day of the week was the pagan day of worship to their gods. The growing Jewish community and even smaller Christian community had always had their day of rest and worship on Saturday, the 7th day of the week as established by the God of the Bible. As mentioned earlier, Constantine the Great, was a sun cult worshiper and decreed that Sunday would be the day of rest for the Roman Empire. This caused a great problem for the Jews and Christians. Constantine soon made it illegal to worship on Saturday. The Jews never acquiesced and suffered greatly. Roman historians record their tragedy for their disobedience to Roman law.

> **Cassius Dio - "As it was, they made an excavation of what are called the days of Saturn and by doing no work at all on those days afforded the Romans an opportunity in this interval to batter down the wall...They build to him a temple that was extremely large and beautiful, except in so far as it was open and roofless, and likewise dedicated to him the day called the day of Saturn, on which, among many other most peculiar observances, they undertake no serious occupation"** (*Roman History*, **37.16.2; 37.16.3**).

> **Frontinus - "The deified Vespasian Augustus attacked the Jews on the day of Saturn, a day on which it is sinful for them to do any business, and so defeated them" (Strategems, book 2).**

What Jewish people were left were placed in ghettos where they were easily controlled by the Romans.

The Christian story was different. Two events occurred that changed the course of the Sabbath. The Catholic Church was established in 313 C.E as a continuation of the Apostolic Church established in 1 C.E. by the disciples of Jesus Christ. (Catholic News Service, 2007) The Apostle Peter was the original Bishop of Rome, the title we now know of as the Pope. (Hitchcock, 2004). After his death, the Christian church had a difficult time being surrounded by the pagan worshipers of Mithras, Baal and Moloch. It evolved to survive and became the wealthy and politically powerful Roman Catholic Church.

OSCAR C. JOHNSON PHD

During the 2nd Century, the bishops began congregating in regional synods to discuss doctrinal and church policy issues. (Chadwick, 1990) Persecution was still a problem for the spread of Christianity due to conflicts with state religion, which was pagan. The Church knew that it had to make some changes to survive so it started to adopt some of the pagan traditions.

In the 4th Century C.E. Emperor Constantine changed from being a sun worshiper to Christian. He knew that there were conflicts between pagans and Christians. He made an observation that pagans throughout the empire worshiped on Sunday and that many Christians in Italy and Greece also worshiped on Sunday. In his efforts to unite paganism and Christianity, he passed his famous Sunday keeping law on March 7, 321 C.E. believing that the passing of this law would create a common platform that would strengthen his empire and unify the religions. Contemporaneously he also made Christianity legal. The Catholic Church leveraged this new legal status to attract pagans to their church by switching their day of worship from Saturday to Sunday. Constantine favored the Roman Catholic Church above all other Christian Churches which was beneficial to the church and advanced its seat of power and influence.

The Catholic Church in an effort to grow its membership, accepted the Sunday day of rest and worship. This was more acceptable to pagans who already worshiped the Sun god on Sunday. This was a brilliant move as more pagans joined the Church giving it more authority. However, this was problematic for traditional apostolic Christians. The Catholic Church never had the authority from God to change the day of worship from the 7th day Sabbath to Sunday. There is no scriptural evidence that ever-made claim to the change and is in direct defiance to the 4th Commandment.

The Jewish people and the early Christians worshiped God by honoring His day of rest after the Creation, which is why they observed the 7th day of the week as their Sabbath day. Jesus Christ and His disciples recognized the 7th day as the Sabbath.


72

The tradition of Sunday worship was spread by the Catholic Church throughout the Roman Empire and most of Europe. Wherever the Romans went, so went the Catholic priest with their policies and traditions. Sunday worship became accepted worldwide as the official day of worship for the Church. Even with the Protestant Reformation led by Martin Luther beginning in 1517 C.E. (Fahlbusch et. al,. 2003), the tradition of Sunday worship continued. Martin Luther was raised and trained Catholic and had been a priest for the Church. Sabbath day worship was initially practiced with the Puritans in America when they migrated from England to escape religious persecution. From the Puritans two groups emerged. These were the Calvinist and Congregationalist. It was these two groups that Sunday worship gained popularity. Both had rational arguments for the change.

One popular rational for Sunday worship is that Jesus was resurrected in the morning of the 1st day of the week. Because the resurrection was a miracle, Jesus followers changed their Sabbath observance to Sunday to remember this was Jesus's day.

Another rational states, since God created the heavens and the Earth on the 1st day of the week and Jesus was resurrected on the 1st day of the week, it should be the day Christians worship. The analogy used is that on the 1st day, God created light to separate it from darkness, Jesus was the light that separates the darkness of sin.

There are those that believe Christians are free from the bondage of the Mosaic Laws. They believe that Jesus abolished Mosaic Law on the cross. For this reason, Christians are not required to observe the Sabbath as a day of worship.

The Bible states emphatically that the Sabbath is the day of worship and commands that we remember it to rest and reflect as we build a stronger relationship with God. Jesus and His disciples observed the Sabbath. He taught not only the Jews but also the Gentiles.

**⁴And he reasoned in the synagogue every sabbath, and persuaded the Jews and the Greeks. (Acts 18:4 KJV)**

Nowhere in the Bible is a declaration of the Sabbath being changed. There is no scriptural reference for a change of the Sabbath. The change to a Sunday worship is an invention of man spearheaded by the Catholic Church. It is commonplace throughout the world, but do not be deceived, Sunday is not the Sabbath.

## The Command

First and foremost, God commands us to "Remember the Sabbath". God does not say to remember any other day. He proceeds to tell us to do all our work in 6 days but give the 7th day to the Lord. The Sabbath begins at sunset on the 6th day and ends on sunset of the 7th day. On the Sabbath day we are to do no work. We should take this time to worship and take time for our fellow man. It is not a day for catching up on chores at home. It is not a time go out and be festive or party.

God created the Sabbath because we need a day of rest. If not for the Sabbath, we would not stop from the demands of this world to give time to God. The Sabbath is a day for fellowship. God wants Christians to assemble and hear His Word preached. It is a day that Christians should do extra prayer and meditation. It is a time to reflect on how small we are in this Universe and how great God is to have created it. Whatever activities that are engaged in should be leisurely and have some relationship to the omnipotence of God and what he does for us.

# THEME II:

# Our Duties To Our Fellow Man

# COMMANDMENT V

Not learning the lessons of the 5<sup>th</sup> Commandment makes it difficult to obey the remainder of the commandments. If one cannot honor their parents, it would also not be possible to honor God. The commandment's deeper importance is the transference of the respect for one's parents to others, children and adults alike. The world today is experiencing widespread disrespect and disregard for our fellow man. Trust is uncommon as a result of exploitation. Fear is as commonplace as distrust due to headlines with multimedia displaying the abuses and atrocities than people enact on each another. Our breakdown in in society begins with failure of the 5<sup>th</sup> Commandment.

The 5<sup>th</sup> Commandment says,

> **<sup>12</sup>Honor thy father and thy mother: that thy days may be long upon the land which the LORD thy God giveth thee. (Exodus 20:12 KJV)**

The 5<sup>th</sup> Commandment is a commandment of promise. The commandment is, to a certain degree, a "bridge" between the commandments regarding our obligations to God and the commandments on how to interrelate with our fellow man. This commandment reminds us of where our character comes from. It is not inherent but is taught to us from our parents who in turn learned from their parents.

> **<sup>20</sup>"My son, observe the commandment of your father And do not forsake the teaching of your mother" (Proverbs 6:20)**

Though this commandment seems to be a casual statement, it has remarkable impact on the intended audience. The inference associated with this commandment brings to mind the role of the parents in teaching the aspects of respect and the children responsibility to learn them. Honoring one's father and mother also honors the Lord. In the Old Testament dispensation, Mosaic Law demanded that children who did not respect their parents should be put to death.

**¹⁵And he that smiteth his father, or his mother, shall be surely put to death. (Exodus 21:15 KJV)**

**¹⁷And he that curseth his father, or his mother, shall surely be put to death. (Exodus 21:17 KJV)**

This was very important to God. Without the lessons of our parents and grandparents we cannot maintain a civil society. The lack of discipline in our modern society has set up a situation where children have lost respect for authority. Parents, mentors, teachers and religious leaders are not willing to take on the challenges to provide structure for children, even though this is what children want. As a result, we have a society where children choose role models from video games, television or movie characters, and typically not the good characters. Children see these glorified criminals as people who deserve respect. They believe that if they act in the same manner, they will get the same respect.

Children from their birth look to their parents for love, security, education and as lawgiver. Children will always limit test to find out what their boundaries are. It is the responsibility of authoritarian figures to provide the discipline and right behavior in them so that they will know how to act as adults when they reach maturity.

The lessons begin at home. The Apostle Paul in his letter to the people of Ephesus wrote,

**¹Children, obey your parents in the Lord: for this is right.**

**²Honour thy father and mother; which is the first commandment with promise;**

**³That it may be well with thee, and thou mayest live long on the earth.**

**⁴And, ye fathers, provoke not your children to wrath: but bring them up in the nurture and admonition of the Lord. (Ephesians 6:1-4 KJV)**

Children's first environment is their home. They have no experience with the outside world and the rules of how to live in it. There is no knowledge of the Lord. It is the responsibility of the parents to teach the Lord's commandments to the children. When it comes to obeying the commandments, children must be taught to obey their parents instantly and without question. Parents must remember to periodically give explanation and reason for obeying the commandments so that the children come to know their God as their parents and ancestors did before them.

If it is expected for the parents to be honored, the parents must be honorable. They must be God fearing and set the example of those who follow the commandments of God and believe and accept Jesus as their savior and Lord. Christian parents realize that they represent God to their children. When they are teaching reverence to their children, they are teaching lessons that will become important as they mature and transfer this reverence to the Lord. Children are observant of what their parents do and hear what their parents are saying, even if they don't act as though they are being attentive. It is important for parents not to be hypocritical. Ultimately, the story of our faith is the foundation that has started with our ancestors and which we are to continue. This begins with honoring our parents and all of those who came before them. The Lord promises reward for following this commandment.

# COMMANDMENT VI

## [13]Thou Shall Not Kill (Exodus 20:13 KJV)

In the legal sense, there are two terms used to describe homicide. These are manslaughter and murder. Neither is lawful but are differentiated by the mindset of the person at the time of the killing. The distinction between the two is very clear. In general terms one is intentional, and the other is not.

## MANSLAUGHTER

A person commits manslaughter when they kill someone without a premeditated intent to kill. Specifically, there is no malice aforethought. This is further defined by voluntary and involuntary.

> **Voluntary manslaughter** is commonly referred to as a "Crime of Passion". These crimes occur when an emotionally provocative circumstance compels a reasonable person to act emotionally and kills in the "heat of the moment". In other words, an individual will kill someone but without premeditation but with strong provocation. The typical scenario involves a spouse coming home to find their spouse cheating on them.

> **Involuntary manslaughter** occurs as a result of criminal negligence or reckless conduct. As in voluntary manslaughter, there is no premeditation. Involuntary manslaughter is an unintentional killing. An example would be shooting a gun into the air and it strikes someone unintentionally, killing them. The more typical example is a drunk or distracted driver causing an accident where someone else is killed as a result. These accidents have their own subcategory known as "vehicular manslaughter".

## MURDER

Similar to manslaughter, murder has two definitions. One is intentional and the other is a disregard for another's life.

**First Degree Murder** – This is the murder that Cain committed against his brother Abel. The elements of this murder include premeditation and intent to kill. This is the most serious of the types of murder.

**Second Degree Murder** – This type of murder occurs intentionally or as a result of disregard to life. An intentional type would be a home invasion where the burglar would be surprised by the homeowner and subsequently kills him/her. The killing was intentional but not premeditated. An example of reckless disregard for life would be an arsonist who is not interested in killing people but only setting a building on fire even though the building is filled with people.

The court system in the United States ranks homicide. The higher the ranking, the more severe the punishment.

1. First-degree murder
2. Second-degree murder
3. Voluntary manslaughter
4. Involuntary manslaughter

The secular criminal justice system adjudicates the intent of the homicide and delivers a punishment. In this system, God's Word is not preeminent, and judgment may or may not be just. Factors that influence the decisions include the notoriety of the charged, the reputation and power of the law firm representing the charged and the manipulation of the Constitution.

For the Christian who follows the commandments, it is understood what God meant when He gave us this commandment. The Kings James Version of the Bible is the most widely used version of the Bible in the world. In its version, the 4th Commandment in Exodus 20:13 states, "Thou Shall Not Kill". (New Bible Dictionary,

1982) The New International Version states "You shall not murder". Hebrew has two words for kill. One is "*harag*" and the other is "*ratzach*". *Harag* translates to kill/slay. *Ratzach* translates to murder. The Kings James version of the Bible interprets the Hebrew to "kill". This was unfortunate because it is a source of moral confusion for many. When the King James version of the Bible was written in the 17th Century, the English language used the words kill and murder synonymously. Most people assume the 6th Commandment is implying murder, but there are many who interpret the commandment to mean the taking of any life. These people have not considered the English language has changed since 1610 C.E. when the King James version of the Bible was written. The fact is, the original Hebrew used the word *Ratzach*. The imperative not to kill is in the context of unlawful killing resulting in bloodguilt. (Greenburg, 1960) This is the guilt associated with wrongfully causing death or shedding blood. So, what did God mean when he wrote this commandment?

First and foremost, let us consider when the first "kill" occurred. The book of Genesis tells us that upon expulsion from the Garden of Eden, God clothed Adam and Eve with animal skins.

**²¹Unto Adam also and to his wife did the Lord God make coats of skins, and clothed them. (Genesis 3:21)**

God killed an animal(s) to provide covering for modesty and protection against the elements. This killing was by design. Animals will kill for food. They do not kill for sport. God allows killing in this sense for Man to have clothing and food. If He didn't Man would be vegetarian. Furthermore, all people would be pacifist. They would not be able to kill even in their own self-defense.

Immanuel Kant's Formula of Universal Law (FUL) is widely considered to be incapable of showing that killing others for the sake of one's convenience is absolutely impermissible. (Allison, 2011)

However, God specifically condemns killing of human beings for nefarious reasons. The Bible gives us the story of the first murder.

**⁵but on Cain and his offering he did not look with favor. So Cain was very angry, and his face was downcast.**

**⁶Then the LORD said to Cain, "Why are you angry? Why is your face downcast?**

**⁷If you do what is right, will you not be accepted? But if you do not do what is right, sin is crouching at your door; it desires to have you, but you must rule over it."**

**⁸Now Cain said to his brother Abel, "Let's go out to the field."[a] While they were in the field, Cain attacked his brother Abel and killed him.**

**⁹Then the LORD said to Cain, "Where is your brother Abel?"**

**"I don't know," he replied. "Am I my brother's keeper?"**

**¹⁰The LORD said, "What have you done? Listen! Your brother's blood cries out to me from the ground.**

**¹¹Now you are under a curse and driven from the ground, which opened its mouth to receive your brother's blood from your hand. (Genesis 4:5-11 NIV)**

Notice that Cain was moved to sin by anger. His anger once conceived, caused him to formulate a plan that led him to kill his brother. God's response to Cain's action was to curse him. This is not what God intended when He killed to clothe Adam and Eve. This was murder.

In the famous "Sermon of the Mount" (the Mount of the Olives), where Jesus gave us the "Lord's Prayer" and the "Beatitudes", Jesus spoke to the masses. He explains His purpose to those who were gathered to hear Him teach.

There are those that think that Jesus changed the 10 Commandments when He ministered to the world. Secular scholars and many modern ministers feel that some of the commandments are antiquated and only applied to people of the Old Testament. They posit the 6th Commandment, murder, at times can be justified. It is their contention that the 6th Commandment is not as dogmatic as it was in ancient Mosaic times. It is not uncommon for a skilled lawyer to get murderers acquitted when they are, what appears to be obvious, guilty of murder. This occurs even when there are eyewitnesses or video evidence of the crime. Less scrupulous lawyers will twist words, blur the truth, lie, confuse and hide or manipulate evidence in some of these cases regardless of reality. In the courts of the secular world, God's law is not preeminent. As a result, Western Civilization is increasingly promoting the dereliction of the Commandments. This has made the Commandments morally irrelevant. The 6th Commandment commands that we consider the life and the welfare of others as we do our own. Unfortunately, it has been demonstrated repeatedly that what is not reasoned murder by the laws of man, has more authority than the Bible.

Nevertheless, Jesus is succinct in His testimony to the world. He is unambiguously clear that there is no change in the message of the 10 Commandments and these laws are with us as long as Heaven and Earth exist. He also condemns any who break these laws. There are no excuses. Jesus wanted the people to know that the Laws of Moses are timeless.

After speaking to the masses, Jesus spoke to His disciples regarding certain commandments. He starts with the 6th Commandment. He explains the deeper meaning of the commandment comprehensively.

> **21"You have heard that it was said by the ancients, 'You shall not murder,'[a] and 'Whoever murders shall be in danger of the judgment.'**
>
> **22But I say to you that whoever is angry with his brother without a cause shall be in danger of the judgment. And whoever says to his brother, 'Raca,' shall be in danger of the Sanhedrin. But**

**whoever says, 'You fool,' shall be in danger of hell fire. (Matthew 5:21-22 MEV)**

Jesus describes how the act of murder can come to be. It starts with desire out of anger. A desire for retaliation. A festering anger is not emotionally healthy and does not allow for a peaceful nor calm spirit. It opens an avenue for Satan to increase greater evil thoughts. Thoughts that promote a malicious imagination. The Apostle James warns us regarding desire in any form.

**[15]Then, after desire has conceived, it gives birth to sin; and sin, when it is full-grown, gives birth to death. (James 1:15 NIV)**

Jesus makes clear the full implication of the 6th Commandment that was written by the finger of God and given to Moses. His extended commentary on the subject makes it clear that the first murder by Cain of his brother Abel had its origins in anger.

Since anger, in most cases, is the genesis of any murder, it should be understood. I say most cases because there are individuals who are sociopathic and murder without conscious or cause. This is mental illness. Regarding anger, it is considered one of the basic human emotions. It is an intense emotional state involving a strong uncomfortable and non-cooperative response to a perceived provocation, hurt or threat (Videbeck, 2006). It is the emotion that initiates the "fight or flight" response, where the sympathetic nervous system prepares the body for action. Anger becomes the predominant feeling behaviorally, cognitively, and physiologically when a person makes the conscious choice to take action to immediately stop the threatening behavior of an outside force (DiGiuseppe & Tafrate, 2006).

## Physiology

Like all emotions, anger originate inside the amygdala. The amygdala identifies threats to comfort and health. When threatened the amygdala can trigger reaction before the cortex (responsible for thought and judgment) can provide a reasoned response to the threat. As the anger emotion builds, neurotransmitters (catecholamines) release their chemicals in a surge of energy, increasing the heart rate, raising blood pressure and increasing respiration. Muscles get increased blood flow in preparation for physical action. Cognitively, attention focuses on the source of the threat to the point where all other thoughts are overwhelmed and repressed. Other neurotransmitters, like adrenaline and noradrenaline, are released to maintain the aroused state.

Though psychologist interpret anger as normal for our survival, uncontrolled anger negatively affect personal or social well-being (Novaco, 2000) Anger reduces our ability to accurately process external stimuli. It reduces our ability to reason rationally. Danger is not as formidable, engagements appear less precarious, unreasonable actions are believed to have a higher probably of success and unfavorable outcomes seem incongruous. An angry person poorly judges risk and frequently make disastrous decisions.

When God said, "Thou shall not kill" He obviously meant murder. Lest anyone should doubt the full meaning of this command, Jesus expanded on the command to define what leads up to the action.

Anger does not produce the righteousness that God demands. If it leads to murder, it leads to death. God wants us to be free of all animosity in our hearts. The Apostle Paul gives us some sage advice.

> [31]**Get rid of all bitterness, rage and anger, brawling and slander, along with every form of malice. (Ephesians 4:31 NIV)**
>
> [26]**"In your anger do not sin" [d]: Do not let the sun go down while you are still angry,**
>
> [27]**and do not give the devil a foothold. (Ephesians 4:26-27 NIV)**

The Bible is not inconsiderate of manslaughter. God realizes that people can kill without intent or by accident.

[1]Then the LORD said to Joshua:

[2]"Tell the Israelites to designate the cities of refuge, as I instructed you through Moses,

[3]so that anyone who kills a person accidentally and unintentionally may flee there and find protection from the avenger of blood.

[4]When they flee to one of these cities, they are to stand in the entrance of the city gate and state their case before the elders of that city. Then the elders are to admit the fugitive into their city and provide a place to live among them.

[5]If the avenger of blood comes in pursuit, the elders must not surrender the fugitive, because the fugitive killed their neighbor unintentionally and without malice aforethought.

[6]They are to stay in that city until they have stood trial before the assembly and until the death of the high priest who is serving at that time. Then they may go back to their own home in the town from which they fled." (Joshua 20:1-6 NIV)

The bottom line is that there is moral killing and there is immoral killing. The word for immoral killing is "murder". And the Commandment clearly means, DO NOT MURDER!

Life is sacred. It is given by God, and God only. No individual has the right to take another person's life arbitrarily or by premeditated means.

# COMMANDMENT VII

**¹⁴Thou shalt not commit adultery. (Exodus 20:14 KJV)**

Like the 6th Commandment, the 7th Commandment should be self-evident. Like the 6th Commandment, the 7th Commandment has much deeper implications and meaning.

Adultery: voluntary sexual intercourse between a married person and a person who is not his or her spouse (Oxford Dictionary). This is how most people will look at this commandment. Obviously, it is self-explanatory.

However, this is not entirely accurate. Under Mosaic Law, adultery had a very narrow definition. It stated that a married man could not have sexual intercourse with a married women or a betrothed woman. Therefore, it was not adultery if the married man had sexual intercourse with an unmarried woman or an unbetrothed woman. It was also not adultery if the woman was not a virgin.

In those ancient times, women were considered more like slaves, a little more than property. Having sexual intercourse with a married women was analogous to exploitation of one's property. A more practical reason to restrict adultery was to prevent possible pregnancies. A child produced as a result of adultery would present a question of parentage. Who could claim fatherhood in this situation? Lineage was critically important to the people of Israel, and they kept meticulous records.

The Jewish people were the chosen people of God. For this reason, God favored, protected and blessed them. The most important reason to prevent adultery was to insure children born were of true

Jewish lineage. If they weren't, they could not enjoy the blessings from God, nor could they contribute or take part in Jewish life and culture.

Not only did adultery cause a problem for parentage, there were also more extensive factors that impacted their society. There were twelve tribes of Israel. Lineage proved which tribe one belonged to. This was important with regard to inheritance of land. It also was important as to which family a child was born into. A child descended from Moses had much more status than from a lesser tribe. Also, if one was not a descendant of Levi, he could not be in the priesthood. Priest could only come from the tribe of Levi, descended from Moses's brother Aaron. Family legacy was exceedingly importantly in Jewish culture. Legacy had to be preserved from generation to generation to the honor of the family name. The importance of genealogy extended to the New Testament. The Old Testament prophesized the Messiah would descend from the line of King David. Meticulous records not only trace Jesus to David but the Apostle Matthew traces Jesus back to Abraham. The Gospel of Luke goes even further and traces Jesus to the first man, Adam. This is the importance of keeping the lineage pure without questions of parentage.

Furthermore, adultery, when realized destroys households. It disrupts the domestic peace and harmony. Adultery dishonors the sanctity of marriage and the bond that marriage entails. It exposes a disrespect that one spouse has for another. Not only does it affect the affronted spouse, it also affects the family as a whole. Children, especially the younger ones, cannot comprehend the implications and emotions involved. They tend to become withdrawn and angry. God made this a commandment because it is a destroyer of families. In this act men and women are equal. A condemnation of adultery was a death sentence by Mosaic Law. Mosaic Law did not tolerate the adulterers. Neither does God.

**¹⁰And the man that committeth adultery with another man's wife, even he that committeth adultery with his neighbour's wife, the adulterer**

**and the adulteress shall surely be put to death. (Leviticus 20:10 KJV)**

God views marriage as a covenant between a man and a woman. This was instituted by God with Adam and Eve. The person who commits adultery has no respect for themselves, their spouse or God.

> [14]**You ask why he no longer accepts them. It is because he knows you have broken your promise to the wife you married when you were young. She was your partner, and you have broken your promise to her, although you promised before God that you would be faithful to her.**

> [15]**Didn't God make you one body and spirit with her?[a] What was his purpose in this? It was that you should have children who are truly God's people. So make sure that none of you breaks his promise to his wife.**

> [16]**"I hate divorce," says the LORD God of Israel. "I hate it when one of you does such a cruel thing to his wife. Make sure that you do not break your promise to be faithful to your wife." (Malachi 2:14-16)**

Contemporary Christians have a much more comprehensive meaning to adultery. Though not uniform in its meaning, adultery will include lustful thinking, lustful words, lustful habits, homosexual sexual intercourse, fornication, whoredom or polygamy. This list is not inclusive but has raised some interesting views. This very broad definition suggests almost any extramarital sex act violates the 7th Commandment.

It is debated whether adultery can be justified or not. A Christian who presumably is guilty of adultery and follows Mosaic Law regarding the subject will typically observe the original law position. If we are expected to follow the original commandment, then shouldn't the commandment be applied in the context of Mosaic Law? This position argues against any expansion of the commandment.

As the morality of society becomes more humanistic, the original law becomes more antiquated in the secular world. The arguments for expansion of the law excludes God's Word in the expanded definition. In doing so, the discussion evolves into whether the 7th Commandment is pertinent in modern society since the reasons, lineage and land inheritance, are not relevant as in the time of Moses. Secularists argue the complexity of the legal system for the need to expand the definition and the ramification of the act of adultery.

What was once considered a crime in every state in the United States, adultery is now only illegal in 21 states. In 16 states adultery is considered a misdemeanor. In 5 states adultery is considered a felony. It is not a crime in 29 states. In the justice system of the United States, we see God's Word is not preeminent when it pertains to adultery.

The Apostle Paul admonishes the Corinthians against sexual immorality.

**[18]Flee from sexual immorality. All other sins a person commits are outside the body, but whoever sins sexually, sins against their own body. (1 Corinthians 6:18 NIV)**

There are those who questions why the definition has been expanded. If we are expected to follow the original commandment, then shouldn't the commandment be applied in the context of Mosaic Law.

These same people will argue that sinful thoughts or words do not parallel the act of adultery. Thinking about having sex with a person you shouldn't have sex with may not be wise, but it's hardly the same thing as the actual act itself — just like thinking about murder isn't the same as murder. (Cline, 2020)

These arguments presume God is solitarily taking into consideration the act of adultery itself. This could be no further from the truth. The Law of Causality is a fundamental principle of science that tries to discover what caused what to happen. For any action, there is a cause. Jesus addresses the cause in His "Sermon of the Mount". To the married person, the cause begins with the eyes. One sees a person that is attractive to them. It is not a sin to appreciate the beauty of the opposite sex. The sin occurs when the attractiveness turns into desire, which in turn becomes lust. It is the lust that is the sin.

> **[27]"You have heard that it was said by them of old time, Thou shalt not commit adultery:**
>
> **[28]But I say unto you, That whosoever looketh on a woman to lust after her hath committed adultery with her already in his heart." (Matthew 5:27-28)**

The 7th Commandment admonishes us to guard our thoughts when admiring someone who is attractive to us. We should not pollute our imaginations with lustful thinking. Nor should we be lured to lustful thoughts with pornographic images or literature, conversations or temptations.

# COMMANDMENT VIII

¹⁵**Thou shalt not steal.** (Exodus 20:15 KJV)

T he 8ᵗʰ Commandment is our third duty to our fellow man. This command represents respect for another's property. In all modern societies, governments recognize private property and social order is based upon it. Anarchy would ensue if governments did not protect the properties rights of every citizen and according to English physician, philosopher and political theorist John Locke, citizens had the right to abolish governments that did not protect this basic right.

Right to ownership has been an instinctual reality since the dawn of man. Secular scholars tell us that a caveman who created his own stone or flint instrument claimed ownership of that implement. If it was taken by force or deception, he would have been victimized. A dishonest act such as this would justify punishment.

The Bible specifically discusses stealing whether it is a person or property.

> ¹⁶**And he that stealeth a man, and selleth him, or if he be found in his hand, he shall surely be put to death. (Exodus 21:16 KJV)**
>
> ¹**If a man shall steal an ox, or a sheep, and kill it, or sell it; he shall restore five oxen for an ox, and four sheep for a sheep. (Exodus 22:1 KJV)**

The 8ᵗʰ Commandment requires us to respect the property of others. To understand the full extent of this commandment, consider what "steal" actually means. Interesting enough, it does not tell us what we aren't supposed to steal. Dennis Prager, the respected nationally, syndicated columnist and radio talk show host, presents an applicable and comprehensive commentary on the topic.

**Stealing of Person** – This commandment was always understood to mean, before anything, we are not allowed to steal human beings. The early rabbinic tradition interpreted this commandment as specifically referring to kidnapping.

Kidnapping people and selling them into slavery, as was done to Africans and others throughout history, is forbidden by the Eighth Commandment. Critics of the Bible who argue the Bible allowed such slavery, and defenders of such slavery who used the Bible, were both wrong.

And lest there be any confusion about this issue, the Torah specifies a person who kidnaps another—particularly when done with the intention of selling the victim into slavery - "shall be put to death."

**Stealing of Property** – This is the most obvious meaning of the commandment. The 8th Commandment is a prohibition against stealing property—and that, in turn, means God sanctifies personal property.

It has been shown over and over that private property, beginning with land ownership, is indispensable to creating a free and decent society. Virtually all tyrannies, especially totalitarian regimes, take away private property rights. And in the ancient and medieval worlds, almost no one had property rights: a few rich people owned all the land.

Then, in nineteenth-century Europe, many socialists argued for confiscating private property and giving it to the "people." Where that advice was followed, in what came to be known as the communist world.

**Stealing Another Person's Reputation, Dignity, Trust, and Intellectual Property** – Another enormously important meaning of the commandment against stealing concerns stealing the many non-material things each person owns: his or her reputation, dignity, trust, and intellectual property.

- Reputation – Stealing a person's good name—whether through libel, slander, or gossip—is a particularly destructive form of theft. It can almost never be fully restored. As Shakespeare put it in *Othello*: "But he that filches from me my good name robs me of that which not enriches him and makes me poor indeed."

- Dignity – The act of stealing a person's dignity is known as humiliation. And humiliating people, especially in public, can do permanent damage, given that dignity may be the most precious thing we own.

- Trust – Stealing a person's trust is known as deceit. Tricking a person into one's way of thinking is deception and stealing. The Hebrew language has a word for this type of stealing, "g'neivatda'at". It means, stealing knowledge or stealing another's mind.

- Intellectual Property – This form of theft includes anything from copying software or films, to downloading music and movies without paying for them, to stealing a person's words (plagiarism). In a major moral statement emphasizing how right and important it is to cite the source of an idea or a quote, the Mishna says, "A person who quotes a statement in the name of the person who stated it brings redemption to the world."

(Prager, 2018)

Most people don't think they are stealing when they take a pen from the office or a towel from a hotel. They don't think they are stealing when they leave early from work or rounding up their expense account receipts. Not returning a borrowed item from a friend or failing to repay a small loan are also examples of stealing. Even so, none of the aforementioned types of stealing are serious in the eyes of most people. This type of stealing though, is a testament of one's character. God is watching and knows our heart. It is as easy not to steal as it is to steal. Obeying this commandment when no one is looking shows the character on one's heart. It shows a respect for someone else's property.

Stealing is dealt with in various ways around the world. Some cultures are more lenient than others, but the common thread is that all societies have some form of punishment.

China – Lethal Injection

Iran – Limb amputation

Iraq – Death Penalty

Mexico – up to 40 years in prison

North Korea – Firing Squad

Turkey – 1 to 10 years in prison

United States – petty theft may result in a small fine and 6 months in jail, grand theft may result in a year or more in prison and a large fine. Repeat of offenses may result in life imprisonment.

An inaction that many people overlook pertains to stealing from God. The Lord has allowed us to be stewards over what is rightfully ours. This was established in the Covenant He made with the people of Israel during the time of Moses. However, they were not allowed to keep what did not belong to them. Specifically, this meant tithes and offerings for the temple and priest. This inaction was stealing from God then and continues today.

> [6]"I the LORD do not change. So you, the descendants of Jacob, are not destroyed.
> [7]Ever since the time of your ancestors you have turned away from my decrees and have not kept them. Return to me, and I will return to you," says the LORD Almighty.
> "But you ask, 'How are we to return?'

> [8]"Will a mere mortal rob God? Yet you rob me.
> "But you ask, 'How are we robbing you?'
> "In tithes and offerings.
>
> [9]You are under a curse—your whole nation—because you are robbing me. (Malachi 3:6-9 NIV)

In the time of Moses, the Levites were the priest and were not permitted to earn an income as they were committed to the work of the Lord 24 hours a day. The people were required to contribute tithes to the temple to provide for the priest. Tithes represented 1/10 of their income.

This requirement has not changed today, yet people tend to not think of it as stealing from God. People believe that they can't afford to tithes. That their worldly financial commitments do not allow leftover money. They rationalize that God would understand that they don't have enough money to tithe. The Apostle Paul discusses this in his second letter to the church in Corinth.

> [10]Now he who supplies seed to the sower and bread for food will also supply and increase your store of seed and will enlarge the harvest of your righteousness. (2 Corinthians 9:10 NIV)
>
> [6]Remember this: Whoever sows sparingly will also reap sparingly, and whoever sows generously will also reap generously. (2 Corinthians 9:6 NIV)

In addition to not stealing from others, we refrain from stealing from God by committing our tithes first before paying our bills or using our funds in a discretionary manner. God has appointed priest to shepherd His people. Failing to support them financially is a contemptuous attitude towards the Covenant that is established between God and us.

The important thing to remember for the believer is that all that we have is from the Lord and belongs to the Lord. We are just stewards, so if He says a portion should be dedicated to support His ministers and priest and for charitable work, we must honor this obligation.

The 8th commandment encompasses all the duties required of the final six commandments. It requires us to respect and honor others person and property. As Jesus commands us,

> **31The second is this: 'Love your neighbor as yourself.' There is no commandment greater than these." (Mark 12:31 NIV)**

To disobey the 8th Commandment not only dishonors God's command but shows no respect for oneself as well as others. It also dishonors God by failing to remain committed to the Covenant by not "returning to Him".

# COMMANDMENT IX

**¹⁶Thou shalt not bear false witness against thy neighbor. (Exodus 20:16 KJV)**

God made Man in His own image. Part of this image is His character. God intends for Man to exhibit His character in behavior and speech. God does not and cannot lie. By fiat, Jesus, His only begotten son, also does not lie.

**¹⁹God is not human, that he should lie, not a human being, that he should change his mind.**
**Does he speak and then not act?**
**Does he promise and not fulfill? (Numbers 23:19 NIV)**

**⁶Jesus saith unto him, I am the way, the truth, and the life: (John 14:6 KJV)**

God wrote this commandment to protect one against calumny of character and to preserve another's reputation. He abhors lying in any form. Man is associated with God by pursuing and asserting the truth.

**²²Lying lips are abomination to the LORD: but they that deal truly are his delight. (Proverbs 12:22 KJV)**

Man born of sin and subject to sinful nature lies and bear false witness with very little thought to the fact that they are lying. Lying has become so invasive in our society that it is difficult to separate the skillful lie from the truth.

Fundamentally, there are three types of lies.

1. Jocose – a lie told to be humorous or jokingly

2. Officious – a lie told for a useful purpose or in benevolence

3. Mischievous – a lie told to injure

Lying begins in the heart. For whatever reason it is spoken. What is spoken is either good or evil. The Apostle James reminds us of the perils of the tongue.

**[8]But the tongue can no man tame; it is an unruly evil, full of deadly poison. (James 3:8 KJV)**

Excluding the mechanical pleasantries, "I'm fine", "Doing well", "Couldn't be better", "Living the dream", "No problem", et cetera, we witness people of prominence, lawyers, politicians, judges, industrial leaders, clergy, professors, newscasters, the list goes on of those who lie in professional settings, courts and churches. The lie misleads deliberately whether for good or bad. This common practice is acceptable though when it leads to a greater good. But is this morally justified?

The German philosopher, Immanuel Kant, proffers an ethical dilemma.

A person runs by you. Moments later another person runs by you with a weapon and asks you if you have seen someone running away just seconds earlier and in what direction were they headed.

In this example there are two options. Option 1: tell the pursuer which way the chased went. Option 2: say you didn't see the person.

If Option 1 is enacted the truth may result in harm or death to the one being chased. If Option 2 is enacted, a lie may save a life. This is the ethical dilemma.

Many would say that Option 2 has a greater moral imperative because it may prevent a harm, regardless of what happen previously. Morally, this option does not allow one to intentionally put someone in a situation where they could be harmed. Option 2 places us in a position to judge. In this scenario, we do not have enough information to make a judgment. Is the person pursuing an officer of the law? Is this person the aggressor? To enact Option 2 is to accept a position of ethical lying. It would preserve the safety of the chased. In other words, to choose to lie in this situation would be a good thing.

For the person who does not consider the welfare of the person being chased and enacts Option 1, they are opting for truth. They have the same information as the person who chose Option 2, which is clearly inadequate to make a judgment. We don't know what the cause is for this situation. We don't know who is right or who is wrong. Nonetheless, absolute moral law to tell the truth compels them to "never lie" regardless of the consequences.

Obviously, there are lies that are malicious and lies that made in jest or amusement. There are "white lies" to spare feelings or propagate trust. There are officious lies that are told to benefit someone and injurious lies that intend to cause harm. It is these disparate types of lies that the morality of lying is the subject of debate among philosophical and religious scholars.

The injunction on lying is embedded in major religions and most homes. Parents teach their children early not to lie. This is continued by scholars and church leaders in perpetually. Yet lying appears habitual and unavoidable.

In the approximate year, 300 C.E. the early Catholic Church Doctor, Saint Augustine of Hippo, wrote a discourse titled "On Lying". In this discourse he asks "whether the definition of a lie includes the intention to deceive. (On Lying, n. 4) Here he questions if every lie is a sin. Though he does not definitively state all lies are sins, he does say that a person should only state what they believe to be true and should not have an intention to deceive.

This was very early in the Catholic Church history and development of church doctrine was only emerging. As the doctrine developed the Magisterium of the Roman Catholic Church defined morality as three elements: the three fonts (the basis for the morality of an act) of morality. An act is immoral if any of the fonts are corrupt. Conversely, if all fonts are virtuous the act is moral. This is not a theological opinion but the official instruction of the Roman Catholic Church.

> Compendium of the Catechism: "The morality of human acts depends on three sources: the object chosen, either a true or apparent good; the intention of the subject who acts, that is, the purpose for which the subject performs the act; and the circumstances of the act, which include its consequences." (Compendium, n. 367)

The three fonts of morality are:

1. Intention – An intention is the agent of action for choosing an act. This is a state mind. The act has an intended objective or end. Malicious intent has a goal to cause damage or harm for evil purpose. A bad intention is immoral and a sin.

2. Moral Object – The end goal of any act is the moral object. It is the moral nature of the act as viewed by God. If the act is inherently structured towards evil results in an end, that is evil. If the act is inherently structured towards virtue, its moral object is good. So we see the act, its makeup and its object are undividable and linked to each other. The morality of the act is determined by the consequence of the act.

3. Circumstances – Every act occurs within a set of circumstances. The circumstance could have occurred in the past. The circumstance could be in the present. A circumstance in the past cannot be altered. A circumstance in the present has a yet to be determined consequence. It is the future circumstances where a chosen act can be determined moral or not. Good or bad consequence outcomes can be realistically predicted at the time the act is chosen.

The Magisterium of the Catholic Church was entrusted with the authority to interpret the Word of God, "whether in its written form or in the form of Tradition" (Storck, 2018). The Magisterium includes the Pope and the college of bishops. (Catechism of the Catholic Church, 85, 100)

Scripture and Tradition "make up a single sacred deposit of the Word of God, which is entrusted to the Church", (Dei Verbum", 2018) and the Magisterium is not independent of this, since "all that it proposes for belief as being divinely revealed is derived from this single deposit of faith." (Catechism, 2018)

The Magisterium addressed sin by separating it into categories. The first was a mortal sin. This is a sin that can lead to damnation. This is a severe or serious sin. A sin of this nature can lead to a separation from God's saving grace if not repented. There are lies that cause so much harm that they are mortal sins according to the Catechism.

The second category of sin is an invention of the Magisterium. The Magisterium did not believe all sin caused damnation. They determined that there is sin that is not so grave they deserved damnation. This type of sin was called a "venial" sin. This sin is an action that should not be done yet does not separate one from God's grace. The Catholic Catechism states venial sins cannot be compounded to collectively constitute a mortal sin. (Librena Editrice Vaticana, 2019)

"White Lies" are sins that are considered in the classification of venial sin. The Magisterium did not believe that all lies were mortal sins. This was partly due the ambiguity of Saint Augustine.

In the book, "The Catechism of Catholic Ethics: A work of Roman Catholic moral theology", the author explains the Catholic opinion.

.021. A venial sin is an act that is not so gravely immoral before God as to be entirely incompatible with true love of God and neighbor. An actual venial sin does not include sufficient culpability to take away the state of grace from the soul, nor to deserve eternal damnation. A venial sin is always in some way contrary to true love of God and neighbor, but to a substantially limited extent. An actual venial sin always includes some culpability and some lack of cooperation with grace, and always deserves some degree of punishment. (Conte, 2011)

Saint Thomas Aquinas advances the work of Saint Augustine regarding the act of lying. He defines lying as "a statement at variance with the mind" and discusses his thoughts on this topic in his greatest work, the Summa Theologica written between 1265 C.E - 1274 C.E. Saint Thomas realizes that Saint Augustine does not resolve the question as to whether or not a false declaration without intent to deceive is a lie in his discourse "On Lying". Saint Augustine discusses various conceivable definitions of lying but does not reconcile to a conclusive definition. Neither does he take a position on the "intent to deceive" question. In "Summa Theologica" he quotes:

> "The desire to deceive belongs to the perfection of lying, but not to its species, as neither does any effect belong to the species of its cause." [Summa Theologica, II-II, 110, 3, Reply to Objection 3.]

Deciphering this quote clarifies its meaning and satisfies the criteria of the fonts. "Desire" in this quote is the intention (1st font) of the act. The "effect" in this quote is the consequence of the circumstance (3rd font). Neither the intention nor the circumstance changes the moral nature, which is defined by the moral object (2nd font). Thus, Saint Thomas believed the act of lying is always immoral, irrespective of intention or circumstances. He believed that this was a "grey" issue where something was bad, but not truly bad. The contrast between the venial and mortal sin is likened to something imperfect to something that is perfect.

Though this contrast exist Saint Thomas believed there were mortal and venial lies. The difference lies in the end goal, the moral object. Ultimately, God is the end. If the lie is serious enough to turn one away from God, it is a mortal sin. If the lie has no intent to deceive and maintains one's relationship with God, it is a venial sin.

"Therefore, when the soul is so disordered by sin as to turn away from its last end, viz. God, to Whom it is united by charity, there is mortal sin; but when it is disordered without turning away from God, there is venial sin." (St. Thomas Aquinas, Summa Theologica, I-II, Q. 72, A. 5.)

To be clear, as Saint Thomas supported the Church position of venial and mortal sin. He fervently believed any lie is sin. The significance of the lie, however, should be considered regarding the moral object or nature of the lie. With the Church's acceptance of the philosophy of Venial versus Mortal sin, it spread this doctrine throughout its realm of influence. As a result, most of the world accepts this philosophy also.

So, the question is, "Can lies be ethical?" An unethical lie is usually easily identified, but quite often ethical lies are subtle and cannot be detected. These are the lies people tell to help someone or protect someone. This type of lying is called Prosocial lying. It is the "White Lie" that is inconsequential in most people's opinion. This type of lie is told to avoid inconveniencing an individual with the reality of the truth. We tell an athlete that they did a great job when their gameplay was mediocre. We tell someone that their presentation was excellent, even though it could have been much better. Many people will say that this type of dishonesty is ethical and moral with no harm associated to it. There are numerous times we try to support someone through Prosocial lying.

"We say lying is wrong in our personal and professional lives, but we often catch ourselves feeling very uncomfortable when we have to tell the truth", says Dr. Emma Levine from the Wharton School of the University of Pennsylvania. Dr. Levine and Dr. Maurice Schweitzer produced a research paper evaluating whether "deception that can sometimes be helpful to other people" (Levine & Schweitzer, 2014) They looked at well-intentioned lies and selfish or meaningless lies. The conclusion to the research observed benevolence to be more important than honesty. In other words, the moral foundation of care possibly has a higher value than the moral foundation of justice.

Social Psychologist Bella DePaulo PhD from the University of Virginia, in a 1996 study, confirmed a theory of Fredrick Nietzche that lying "is a condition of life". Her research showed that both men and women lie in approximately a fifth of their social exchanges lasting 10 or more minutes; over the course of a week, they deceive about 30 percent of those with whom they interact one-on-one (Komet, 2016). She also noted that most people lie once or twice a day.

Venial sin in general created a convenient luxury for Man to be lax in upholding the laws of God. The concept of venial sin has saturated the religious establishment as well as the secular world. Unfortunately, like most things conceived by Man, the concept is not Biblical and is a paradigm of the world and not of God.

The Bible is unambiguous when it pertains to lying. Lying is the first sin committed in the world and was committed by Satan, previously known as the angel Lucifer. Satan lied to Eve about God's intent in the Garden of Eden. This lie led to the Original Sin and set the nature of all succeeding generations of Man.

God hates lying in any form. This includes equivocating, maligning, pretending, fraud or deception against one's neighbor. Lying not only hurts others it hurts the person who is lying. It diminishes their integrity while destroying trust from others. Most importantly, lying will jeopardize one's relationship with God and risk their salvation.

> **⁶you will destroy those who speak lies; the LORD abhors the bloodthirsty and deceitful man. (Psalm 5:6 MEV)**

The Apostle Luke gives us the story of a couple, Ananias and Sapphira, who lied and the consequence:

> **¹But a certain man named Ananias, with Sapphira his wife, sold a possession,**

²And kept back part of the price, his wife also being privy to it, and brought a certain part, and laid it at the apostles' feet.

³But Peter said, Ananias, why hath Satan filled thine heart to lie to the Holy Ghost, and to keep back part of the price of the land?

⁴Whiles it remained, was it not thine own? and after it was sold, was it not in thine own power? why hast thou conceived this thing in thine heart? thou hast not lied unto men, but unto God.

⁵And Ananias hearing these words fell down, and gave up the ghost: and great fear came on all them that heard these things.

⁶And the young men arose, wound him up, and carried him out, and buried him.

⁷And it was about the space of three hours after, when his wife, not knowing what was done, came in.

⁸And Peter answered unto her, Tell me whether ye sold the land for so much? And she said, Yea, for so much.

⁹Then Peter said unto her, How is it that ye have agreed together to tempt the Spirit of the Lord? behold, the feet of them which have buried thy husband are at the door, and shall carry thee out. ¹⁰Then fell she down straightway at his feet, and yielded up the ghost: and the young men came in, and found her dead, and, carrying her forth, buried her by her husband. (Acts 5:1-10)

Ananias and Sapphira not only lied but they violated the 8th Commandment. They conspired to steal from God. But God sees all things and knows our hearts.

In the Revelation of Jesus Christ, the Apostle John gives us His inspired word regarding the destiny of liars.

**[8]But the fearful, and unbelieving, and the abominable, and murderers, and whoremongers, and sorcerers, and idolaters, and all liars, shall have their part in the lake which burneth with fire and brimstone: which is the second death. (Revelation 21:8 KJV)**

The 9th Commandment is given to safeguard one against defamation of character and to sustain an honest man's reputation. The spiritual applications of this commandment are enormous in effect. God is the ultimate standard of righteousness and truth. The honest person will always acknowledge this truth and endeavor to speak the truth.

The person that lies is concerned more about what others thinks of them than what God thinks of them. Their self-esteem and sense of importance, in the presence of other people, dominates their sense of morality. The Apostle John saw this firsthand when Jesus arrived in Jerusalem. There were many who said they believed in Him, yet they were afraid to greet Him for fear of the Pharisees and Sanhedrin.

**[42]Nevertheless among the chief rulers also many believed on him; but because of the Pharisees they did not confess him, lest they should be put out of the synagogue:**
**[43]For they loved the praise of men more than the praise of God. (John 12:42-43 KJV)**

God does not lie. If he told even one lie, then the Bible categorically fails. There would be no trust in any statement He or His son, Jesus could make without contestation. He would be no different than Satan who committed the first lie.

**[19]God is not human, that he should lie, not a human being, that he should change his mind. (Numbers 23:19 NIV)**

Jesus tells us He is the truth (John 14:6), so the expectation of His followers is to be people of truth. On His Sermon on the Mount, Jesus explains,

**³⁷But let your communication be, Yea, yea; Nay, nay: for whatsoever is more than these cometh of evil. (Matthew 5:37 KJV)**

We must remember our moral objects. We must guard our tongues. God condemns those who hold back the truth. Lies of any type will be remembered by Jesus our judge and God.

# COMMANDMENT X

**¹⁷Thou shalt not covet thy neighbour's house, thou shalt not covet thy neighbour's wife, nor his manservant, nor his maidservant, nor his ox, nor his ass, nor any thing that is thy neighbour's. (Exdous 20:17 KJV)**

In the English language, covet, is an intransitive verb meaning

1:    to wish for earnestly //*covet* an award

2:    to desire (what belongs to another) inordinately or culpably //The king's brother *coveted* the throne.

3:    to feel inordinate desire for what belongs to another

(Merriam-Webster Dictionary)

In general terms, covetousness is an unreasonable desire for something that is possessed by another. Unlike the 6th, 7th, 8th and 9th Commandments, this commandment is not concerned with the action of sin unaccompanied. Coveting includes thoughts, feelings, inclinations and desires that come from within. It is part of that nature of sin whether we may need it or not. The problem with coveting is that it cannot be satiated. The person who covets will always want more. A person who is occupied with seeking possessions of this world will stop seeking the kingdom of God.

Coveting starts as a desire for something. This in itself is not sinful. Work hard and gain the resources to purchase the object of desire. The sin occurs when the desire becomes unreasonable or inordinate. Desire is now covetousness. The person now wants possession any way they can get it. Once this takes hold the person is in danger of moving to obtain the object of their desire unlawfully.

Jesus talking to His disciples list the sins that come from within and tells them to guard against them.

> **22Thefts, covetousness, wickedness, deceit, lasciviousness, an evil eye, blasphemy, pride, foolishness: (Mark 7:223 KJV)**

Having desire for these things corrupt the heart and is a sin even if not acted upon. Covetousness is a vice that inclines towards sin. These sins are of Pride, of Flesh, of Concupiscence (sexual desire) or of Avarice (materialism). It is opportunistic and turns affections to divisions, it fills the mind with evil thoughts, it changes one's conduct. Jesus list covetousness amongst the sins that makes a person unclean. A person overwhelmed with covetousness is no longer content with their life. Thus, they are unhappy and make everyone around them unhappy.

The 7th chapter from the Book of Joshua gives us a story of covetousness.

> **18Joshua had his family come forward man by man, and Achan son of Karmi, the son of Zimri, the son of Zerah, of the tribe of Judah, was chosen.**
>
> **19Then Joshua said to Achan, "My son, give glory to the LORD, the God of Israel, and honor him. Tell me what you have done; do not hide it from me."**
>
> **20Achan replied, "It is true! I have sinned against the LORD, the God of Israel. This is what I have done:**
>
> **21When I saw in the plunder a beautiful robe from Babylonia,[a] two hundred shekels[b] of silver and a bar of gold weighing fifty shekels,[c] I coveted them**

and took them. They are hidden in the ground inside my tent, with the silver underneath."

²²So Joshua sent messengers, and they ran to the tent, and there it was, hidden in his tent, with the silver underneath.

²³They took the things from the tent, brought them to Joshua and all the Israelites and spread them out before the LORD.

²⁴Then Joshua, together with all Israel, took Achan son of Zerah, the silver, the robe, the gold bar, his sons and daughters, his cattle, donkeys and sheep, his tent and all that he had, to the Valley of Achor.

²⁵Joshua said, "Why have you brought this trouble on us? The LORD will bring trouble on you today."

Then all Israel stoned him, and after they had stoned the rest, they burned them.

²⁶Over Achan they heaped up a large pile of rocks, which remains to this day. Then the LORD turned from his fierce anger. Therefore that place has been called the Valley of Achor[d] ever since. (Joshua 7:18-26 NIV)

In the aftermath of the conquering of Jericho, Achan disobeyed the command of God to not take anything from the victory. Achan not only took things from Jericho, but he lied about it. He then tells his family and entices them to be complicit in his crime. Upon repeated interrogatory, He continues his lie until it becomes too great a burden, and he confesses. He states that he took clothes and money out of covetousness.

Achan violated the 8th, 9th and 10th Commandments is his sin. He coveted which led to theft, which to lies and deception. Though he confessed in the end, there were consequences for his action. Achan and his whole family were stoned to death, burned and made into a rock memorial as a reminder for people to obey God's commandments.

In the New Testament, Jesus teaches His disciples a more subtle form of covetousness.

> **¹⁵And he said unto them, Take heed, and beware of covetousness: for a man's life consisteth not in the abundance of the things which he possesseth.**
>
> **¹⁶And he spake a parable unto them, saying, The ground of a certain rich man brought forth plentifully:**
>
> **¹⁷And he thought within himself, saying, What shall I do, because I have no room where to bestow my fruits?**
>
> **¹⁸And he said, This will I do: I will pull down my barns, and build greater; and there will I bestow all my fruits and my goods.**
>
> **¹⁹And I will say to my soul, Soul, thou hast much goods laid up for many years; take thine ease, eat, drink, and be merry.**
>
> **²⁰But God said unto him, Thou fool, this night thy soul shall be required of thee: then whose shall those things be, which thou hast provided?**
>
> **²¹So is he that layeth up treasure for himself, and is not rich toward God. (Luke 12:15-21 KJV)**

In this parable, there is a brother who is asking Jesus to arbitrate between he and his brother regarding inheritance. He wants Jesus to make his brother share the inheritance with him. In those days the tradition was for the firstborn to receive the inheritance from the father. The brother who wants a share is not in possession of the inheritance and is not entitled to anything. His brother is the owner of the inheritance. Rather than arbitrate, Jesus addresses the root problem: covetousness. Jesus admonishes the person and voices loudly that life is more than the abundance of possessions.

Jesus continues with the Parable of the Rich Fool. This was a man who was blessed by the Lord and his lands produced plentifully. Like most people, he did not acknowledge God for his good fortune and instead of using his wealth to further increase the will of God, he invested it in himself. He built larger barns to accumulate more wealth and he planned for a retirement where he did not have to do any more labor. Nowhere in his thinking was the source of his prosperity, God. The rich man died that night. All the treasures in his possession did not bring him closer to God.

There are two points to this parable. The first is that we should not let money become our master. Once it does, we no longer serve the Lord. In this parable the rich man doesn't think of God, nor did he take Him into consideration. God is completely absent from the plans the rich man is making for his present and for his future on Earth. This person is arrogantly thinking that he is the master of his circumstances. He couldn't see that life doesn't end with death, and that the soul surpasses mortality and lives on into perpetuity.

Besides, who is this money for once we die? Who deserves the accumulated possessions that weren't earned? Are these possessions to be points of contention and cause greater harm? These situations occur all the time when undeserved wealth is debated over. Unfortunately, more times than not, wealth left behind is underappreciated.

The second point of this parable considers amassing wealth for ourselves. In this case the covetousness lies in the fact of always wanting more. It includes the coveting of power and status. He didn't think of anyone but himself. It never occurred to him to give, to contribute, to offer of his abundance to others. This form of covetousness takes from God and claims the credit for themselves. If we are blessed by God, this blessing should be shared with others. God gives to us to honor Him. First, we need to give back to God by giving Him the first fruits of our increase. We should also help those who are less fortunate than we are. If we honor God with what He has provided us, He will bless us with more that we can honor Him with more. In his letter to the Corinthians, the Apostle Paul summarizes this point appropriately.

[6]Remember this: Whoever sows sparingly will also reap sparingly, and whoever sows generously will also reap generously.

[7]Each of you should give what you have decided in your heart to give, not reluctantly or under compulsion, for God loves a cheerful giver.

[8]And God is able to bless you abundantly, so that in all things at all times, having all that you need, you will abound in every good work.

[9]As it is written:

"They have freely scattered their gifts to the poor; their righteousness endures forever."[a]

[10]Now he who supplies seed to the sower and bread for food will also supply and increase your store of seed and will enlarge the harvest of your righteousness.

[11]You will be enriched in every way so that you can be generous on every occasion, and through us your generosity will result in thanksgiving to God.

[12]This service that you perform is not only supplying the needs of the Lord's people but is also overflowing in many expressions of thanks to God.

[13]Because of the service by which you have proved yourselves, others will praise God for the obedience that accompanies your confession of the gospel of Christ, and for your generosity in sharing with them and with everyone else.

[14]And in their prayers for you their hearts will go out to you, because of the surpassing grace God has given you.

**¹⁵Thanks be to God for his indescribable gift! (2 Corinthians 9:6–15 NIV)**

Saul of Tarsus was born into wealth. Saul of Tarsus, the Pharisee (Hasidim or Pious One), was the Jews Jew. Saul knew the Mosaic Laws better than almost everyone. He had position and status. After his conversion, he renounced his wealth and position. He turned his back to the legalism associated with the Jewish religious construct. He changed his name to Paul and committed himself to the Gospel of Christ. Paul the Apostle was poor. Paul the Apostle had no status, was beaten, stoned, tortured, chained and imprisoned. The Apostle Paul knew that people would covet whether they were rich or poor.

> **⁷What then shall we say? That the law is sin? By no means! Yet if it had not been for the law, I would not have known sin. For I would not have known what it is to covet if the law had not said, "You shall not covet."**
>
> **⁸But sin, seizing an opportunity through the commandment, produced in me all kinds of covetousness. For apart from the law, sin lies dead. (Romans 7:7-8 ESV)**

He also realized that the deleterious effects of covetousness can be averted if one learns to be content. God is sovereign and His providence provides everything that the believer needs. The Apostle Paul told Timothy, his protégé, that he learned to be content in any situation. Covetousness leads one to desire, and desire causes suffering, "But godliness with contentment is great gain" (1 Timothy 6:6 KJV). He knew that if we needed more God would provide more. Every Christian should keep this in mind before he starts to covet what may belong to others.

Remember, the covetousness is an excessive and unwarranted desire. It is a sin of the heart that doesn't require action. Once one starts to desire irrationally, the sin occurs. What this sin will do is act as a conduit to actions that could lead to violation of multiple other commandments of God. Conceding material possessions to become more significant than the Lord and to covet them in our lives, makes us guilty of idolatry.

A real-life scenario could transpire like this:

A person covets money so much that his whole being is devoted to the process of making more of it. In coveting money, this person breaks the 10th Commandment. The 1st and 2nd Commandments have also been broken since money has become the God and idol to this person. Acting on the covetousness can extend to become crimes against Man's law and more importantly crimes against Gods law. If by fraud or deception money is gained, the 8th and 9th Commandments are violated.

This is not a far-fetched scenario. This happens every day. Mostly likely, you have seen or know someone that is a slave to money and does whatever it takes to get it. As you can see, violating one commandment can quickly become a disastrous breakdown of multiple Laws of God. At the Sermon on the Mount, Jesus speaks to the worship of two masters, God or Mammon (money).

> **13No servant can serve two masters: for either he will hate the one, and love the other; or else he will hold to the one, and despise the other. Ye cannot serve God and mammon.**
>
> **14And the Pharisees also, who were covetous, heard all these things: and they derided him. (Luke 16:13-14 KJV)**

Throughout the Bible the prophets of old, the apostles and Jesus warns us not to covet. It destroys the heart causing separation from the grace of God. One who covets the possessions of another is not being grateful or content. Their motivation is pure greed. The 10th Commandment added depth to motives of the heart. It exposes the greed that initiated with Eve in the Garden of Eden, when she wanted the knowledge of God. Disobedience to this commandment can lead to multiple breaches of other commandments. Even King Solomon, the smartest man in the world warned against the dangers of covetousness.

> [10]**Whoever loves money never has enough; whoever loves wealth is never satisfied with their income. This too is meaningless. (Ecclesiastes 5:10 NIV)**

King Solomon is aware that greed will never be satisfied. There will always be a desire to have more whether it is needed or not.

> [27]**"He that is greedy of gain, troubleth his own house" (Proverbs 15:27 KJV)**

My fellow Christians, be content with what the Lord has provided for you. He knows what you need. It is not what you store in this earthly existence, which is passing, but what treasures you store in heaven.

> [33]**But seek ye first the kingdom of God, and his righteousness; and all these things shall be added unto you. (Matthew 6:33 KJV)**

Of all the lessons given in the Bible, the 10 Commandments or the Laws of Moses are the best known and most recognizable. The Ten Commandments are the ultimate manifestation of God's will. They are evidence of a covenant between God and the Jewish people. These commandments were given to Man to guide them in developing a relationship with their Creator. In the New Testament, Jesus summarizes the 10 Commandments into two statements.

> [30]**And thou shalt love the Lord thy God with all thy heart, and with all thy soul, and with all thy mind, and with all thy strength: this is the first commandment.**
>
> [31]**And the second is like, namely this, Thou shalt love thy neighbour as thyself. There is none other**

**commandment greater than these. (Mark 12:30-31 KJV)**

The Mount Sinai Text of the Old Testament are given to the Jewish people from the written hand of God. He gives these commandments as instructions on building a relationship with Him and how to comport oneself among other humans. Through the Bible there are many laws that have consequences for disobedience, but if you notice, the commandments do not come with consequences. God presents the commandments without specific retributions for disobedience. He gives us the choice to follow His decrees or not. To choose right from wrong, good from sin. God could enforce His will, but that doesn't create love for Him. We would be a species of robots with no understanding of Gods will.

To not follow the 10 Commandments is to sin. If one does sin, they do it by choice. It cannot be passed on to someone, nor can anyone give another their sin. God wants us to righteousness. That is why he gave us the commandments. That is why Jesus endeavored to clarify the commandments. In the end, sin will separate us from the grace of God and jeopardize our salvation.

> **[20]The soul that sinneth, it shall die. The son shall not bear the iniquity of the father, neither shall the father bear the iniquity of the son: the righteousness of the righteous shall be upon him, and the wickedness of the wicked shall be upon him. (Ezekiel 18:20 KJV)**

# CONCLUSION

I n 2013, Nobel Peace Prize laureate Lech Walesa, called for a new 10 Commandments. He proposed the world needed a new man made 10 Commandment that to that all could embrace. These commandments would strongly promote human interest and weakly endorse Judeo-Christian spirituality. It would be a Secularist 10 Commandments. Walesa wanted to bridge the gap between believers and nonbelievers: a guide that transcended religious belief. In proposing a secular 10 Commandments, he knew that a complete rewriting of the God written 10 Commandments would be required, but he believed that this would unite the world under one basic universal set of principles. At a summit of Nobel Laureates in Warsaw, he stated,

> **"We need to agree on common values for all religions as soon as possible, a kind of secular Ten Commandments on which we will build the world of tomorrow,"**

Though he made this proposal, he did not present what the tenets would be.

Today there is no codified Secular Humanist 10 Commandments. Various groups have presented different versions without universal agreement. However, all versions embrace all or some philosophies that include, affirmation of human worth and dignity, reason, compassion, morality, ethics, democracy, scientific inquiry, naturalism, and critical thinking. What is universal among the humanist, is that there is no reference to a divine creator. I present a few examples of Secular Humanist forms of the 10 Commandments.

## American Humanist Association Center for Education

### The 10 Commitments

1) **Critical Thinking** – I will practice good judgment by asking questions and thinking for myself.

2) **Ethical Development** – I will always focus on becoming a better person.

3) **Peace and Social Justice** – I will help people solve problems and handle disagreements in ways that are fair for everyone.

4) **Service and Participation** – I will help my community in ways that let me get to know the people I'm helping.

5) **Empathy** – I will consider other people's thoughts, feelings, and experiences.

6) **Humility** – I will be aware of my strengths and weaknesses, and appreciate the strengths and weaknesses of others.

7) **Environmentalism** – I will take care of the Earth and the life on it.

8) **Global Awareness** – I will be a good neighbor to the people who share the Earth with me and help make the world a better place for everyone.

9) **Responsibility** – I will be a good person—even when no one is looking—and own the consequences of my actions.

10) **Altruism** – I will help others in need without hoping for rewards.

https://thehumanist.wpenginepowered.com/wp-content/uploads/2019/09/ten_committments_poster.pdf

## Humanist

1) Be open-minded and be willing to alter your beliefs with new evidence. (Jeremy Jimenez)

2) Strive to understand what is most likely to be true, not to believe what you wish to be true. (Matthew Main)

3) The scientific method is the most reliable way of under-standing the natural world. (Isaiah Jackson)

4) Every person has the right to control of their body. (Chris Lager)

5) God is not necessary to be a good person or to live a full and meaningful life. (John Roso)

6) Be mindful of the consequences of all your actions and recognize that you must take responsibility for them. (Jamie Andrews)

7) Treat others as you would want them to treat you, and can reasonably expect them to want to be treated. Think about their perspective. (Carol Fly)

8) We have the responsibility to consider others, including future generations. (Michael Marr)

9) There is no one right way to love. (Eli Chisholm)

10) Leave the world a better place than you found it. (Maury McCoy)

*"Atheist Mind, Humanist Heart: Rewriting the Ten Commandments for the Twenty-first Century." Lex Bayor and John Figdor*

## Creation Ministries International

### The New (secular) Ten Commandments

1) Do not do to others what you would not want them to do to you.

2) In all things, strive to cause no harm.

3) Treat your fellow human beings, your fellow living things, and the world in general with love, honesty, faithfulness and respect.

4) Do not overlook evil or shrink from administering justice, but always be ready to forgive wrongdoing freely admitted and honestly regretted.

5) Live life with a sense of joy and wonder.

6) Always seek to be learning something new.

7) Test all things; always check your ideas against the facts, and be ready to discard even a cherished belief if it does not conform to them.

8) Never seek to censor or cut yourself off from dissent; always respect the right of others to disagree with you.

9) Form independent opinions on the basis of your own reason and experience; do not allow yourself to be led blindly by others.

10) Question everything.

*The New Ten Commandments, www.patheos.com/blogs/daylightathe-ism/essays/the-new-ten-commandments, accessed 13/6/2013.*

## Odyessy Online

### The 10 Secular Commandments

1) Never kill any sentient being except when in direct and immediate danger, or when you have probable cause that killing them would be merciful.

2) Never torture anyone.

3) Never threaten jihad or hate crimes against people of faith (or any other group).

4) Never injure someone except in a consensual fight with agreed conditions or a direct and immediate danger.

5) Never keep someone in emotional torment for extended periods.

6) Never take someone else's work or possessions as your own.

7) Never buy, sell, or own a person unless that person explicitly states their compliance without coercion.

8) Never be sexually unfaithful, coercive, or non-consensually forceful.

9) Never shame someone for their body, race, heritage, or sexual thoughts or actions except those banned in #8.

**10)** Never overindulge without helping others in your community who are more in need than you are

https://www.theodysseyonline.com/the-ten-secular-commandments

As you can see, there is no consensus on what should be included in the 10 secular commandments. They are similar in some respects but totally different in others. With the variation of the secular commandments, those without belief have the options to pick and choose which commandments are pertinent to their lives. Therefore, they would only be accountable to themselves. King David tells us the futility of man-made commandments.

**¹Unless the LORD builds the house, They labor in vain who build it; (Psalms 127:1 NKJV)**

In the eyes of this Christian, to adopt another 10 Commandments would be heretical. The 10 Commandments were written by the finger of God and written in His Word, the Bible. His Word cannot be tampered with.

**¹⁸[a] For I testify to everyone who hears the words of the prophecy of this book: If anyone adds to these things, [b]God will add to him the plagues that are written in this book;**

**¹⁹and if anyone takes away from the words of the book of this prophecy, God[c] shall take away his part from the [d]Book of Life, from the holy city, and from the things which are written in this book. (Revelations 22:18-19 NKJV)**

# FINAL THOUGHTS

God gave us the 10 Commandments as His laws for man. All the Mosaic Laws that followed are interpretations as they relate to the Gods laws. The prophets of the Old Testament and leaders of the Israeli people referred to these divine laws to remind the people of the will of God and to help guide the people in righteous living.

In the New Testament Jesus and the Apostles continued to refer to the 10 Commandments throughout their ministries. Thus, the laws have never changed. Those who truly accept these tenets will be changed forever. The commandments will not be written on tablets of stone but on the tablets of their hearts.

The Psalmist King David accepted the tenets of the 10 Commandments. Such was his love for the Lord.

> **10With my whole heart I have sought You; Oh, let me not wander from Your commandments**
>
> **11Your word I have hidden in my heart, That I might not sin against You.**
>
> **12Blessed *are* You, O LORD! (Psalm 119:10-12 NKJV)**

# REFERENCE

Allison H. E. (2011) Kant's Groundwork for the Metaphysics of Morals: A Commentary. Oxford: OUP.

Catechism of the Catholic Church - IntraText". www.vatican.va. Retrieved 2018-08-16.

Catholic News Service.: "Vatican congregation reaffirms truth, oneness of Catholic Church".. Archived from the original on 10 July 2007. *Retrieved 17 March 2012.*

Christian Forum.: Saturday is the FIRST day of the week NOT the SEVENTH!

https://www.christianforums.com/threads/saturday-is-the-first-day-of-the-week-not-the-seventh.8080841/Sep. 2018

Cline, Austin. "Thou Shalt Not Commit Adultery." Learn Religions, Oct. 29, 2020, learnreligions.com/seventh-commandment-thou-shalt-not-commit-adultery-250906.

"Dei verbum". www.vatican.va. *Retrieved 2018-08-16.*

Drazi, Israel.: (2009). Maimonides and the Biblical Prophets. Gefen Publishing House Ltd. p. 209.

Edwards, M.: Bible Studies. FaithWriters. Sept. 2015https://www.faithwriters.com/article-details.php?id=181435

Exodus 20:1–21, Deuteronomy 5:1–23, Ten Commandments, New Bible Dictionary, Second Edition, Tyndale House, 1982 pp. 1174–1175

Falk, Michael (19 March 1999). "Astronomical names for the days of the week". Journal of the Royal Astronomical Society of Canada. 93 (1999–06): 122–133. Bibcode:1999JRASC..93..122F.

Grossman, Cathy Lynn.: "Americans get an 'F' in religion," USA Today, March 14, 2007, accessed August 11, 2016, http://www.usatoday.com/news/religion/2007-03-07-teaching-religion-cover_N.htm.

Greenberg M., in: Sefer Yovel Y. Kaufmann (1960), 5–28; idem, in: IDB, 1 (1962), S.V.; K. Koch, in: VT, 12 (1962), 396–416; J. Milgrom, Studies in Levitical Terminology, 1 (1970), 22–33, 56–69.

Komet, A.: The Truth About Lying. Psychology Today. published May 1, 1997 - last reviewed on June 9, 2016

Levine, Emma and Schweitzer, Maurice E., Are Liars Ethical? On the Tension between Benevolence and Honesty (2014). Journal of Experimental Social Psychology, 53, 107-117., Available at SSRN: https://ssrn.com/abstract=2910061

Prager D.:4 Things You Never Knew "Thou Shalt Not Steal" Applied To. The Rational Bible. April 4, 2018. Salem Web Network. https://www.biblestudytools.com/bible-study/explore-the-bible/4-things-you-never-knew-thou-shalt-not-steal-applied-to.html

Schaff, Philip (1884). History of the Christian Church Vol. III. Edinburgh: T&T Clark. p. 380. Retrieved 15 March 2019.

Smith M.: British Christians split on whether four of the ten commandments are still important principles to live by. YouGov,UK. October 25, 2017

Storck, Thomas.: What is the Magisterium? www.ignatiusinsight.com. Retrieved 2018-08-16.

Watson, Thomas.: The Sixth Commandment. Bible Hub.

https://biblehub.com/library/watson/the_ten_command-ments/2_6_the_sixth_commandment.htm

# BIBLIOGRAPHY

Andrews JN.: History of the Sabbath and First Day of the Week. Teach Services, Incorporated. 1998. ISBN: 1572581007, ISBN13:9781572581074

Chadwick, Henry.: (1990). "The Early Christian Community". In McManners, John (ed.). The Oxford Illustrated History of Christianity. Oxford University Press. pp. 20–61. ISBN 0-19-822928-3.

Conte, Ronald.: The Catechism of Catholic Ethics: A work of Roman Catholic moral theology. Catholic Planet (April 12, 2011. ASIN: B004WE7K6C

DiGiuseppe, Raymond, Tafrate, Raymond Chip.: Understanding Anger Disorders, Oxford University Press, 2006, pp. 133–159.

Fahlbusch, Erwin, and Bromiley, Geoffrey William (2003). The Encyclopedia of Christianity, Volume 3. Grand Rapids, Michigan: Eerdmans. p. 362.

Grimm, Jacob (2004). Teutonic Mythology. Courier Corporation. pp. 122–123. ISBN 978-0-486-43546-6.

Hitchcock, Geography of Religion (2004), p. 281, quote: "Some (Christian communities) had been evangelized by Peter, the disciple Jesus designated as the founder of his church. Once the position was institutionalized, historians looked back and recognized Peter as the first pope of the Christian church in Rome"

Libreria Editrice Vaticana.: Catechism of the Catholic Church (2nd ed.). 2019. Paragraph 1863.

Novaco, Raymond W.: Anger, Encyclopedia of Psychology, Oxford University Press, 2000

R. C. Sproul: What is Reformed Theology?: Understanding the Basics (ed. Baker Books, 2016) - ISBN: 9781585586523

Steve Singleton: Multi-Index to the Law of Moses. E-book (2007-005) Videbeck, Sheila L. (2006). Psychiatric Mental Health Nursing (3rd ed.). Lippincott Williams & Wilkins. ISBN 9780781760331.

www.ingramcontent.com/pod-product-compliance
Lightning Source LLC
Chambersburg PA
CBHW060240030426
42335CB00014B/1546